Those Were The Days

Memories of Elsie Lillian Florence (Reed) Gentry

with

Addendum and Photographs

William Vernon Reed

Dictated to:

Elsie Ellen Florence (Reed) Gentry who wrote the story
Eugene Greer Gentry, also a writer, for permission
Grandparents, Great Grandparents and parents
of "doubting Thomas's"

Text verbatim.

Author
Elsie Lillian Florence (Reed) Gentry

Pictures and additional information contributed by
William Vernon Reed
Those Were The Days
56 South 33rd Ave
St. Cloud, MN 56301-3722
e-mail: genenatrace@charter.net
www.thosewerethedaysbook.com

ISBN: 1-934478-08-3
ISBN13: 978-1-934478-08-0

Printed in the United States of America by
Sunray Printing Solutions
25123 22nd Ave
St. Cloud, MN 56301-9189
1-888-253-8808

Preface

This story "THOSE WERE THE DAYS" was written by Elsie Lillian Florence (Reed) Gentry in the early 1960's. An interesting story of the late 1800's and early 1900's. The original limited addition is in the Cokato Museum and the Wright County Museum, Some of the family have copies.

You might ask, "why promote this book?" To answer your question. I ask "why are you interested in history?" Its said, "if you are not interested in the past you are not interested in the future."

Every day you see people trying to reinvent the wheel: they try because they don't know it has already been done. Their efforts would be put to better use trying to improve something that has already been done. There are examples in my family of improvements that were made, but that's another story.

Any one who reads this book will come away with a better knowledge of how it was in the good old days. There are grand parents who have told their young grand children and even great grand children about things they have done in their youth and are told," I don't believe it". They have always had electricity, hot and cold water, ice cubes, radios, TV, E-mail , and cell phones let alone telephones (very rare in her day) to name a few. Many came into use in the past 75 years or less.

Most grand parents will never record this type of information for their decedents, but would honestly like them to know that their life was not just a nice bed of roses, with lots of thorns to overcome. Most grandparents will relate to experiences in this story as they are very similar to their own. This is all fact, not a made up story, it was lived by my Aunt Elsie.

I am the only living nephew on the Reed side. (I have added family pictures from available albums, comments in parentheses and information relative to the story).

This story was written by my Aunt, I have put together the text verbatim, adding pictures and related information which I feel make her book more interesting and clarifies some of the text that could be an issue, many would skip over and not research the true meaning.

I also feel that her efforts should be in the Library of Congress in Washington D.C. I want her desires fulfilled "I am putting this in writing so that my grand-children and mayhap my great grand children will read and wonder what made us happy in those years long ago".

Set back and enjoy the things that transpired a century ago.

The only living child of the author, Eugene Greer Gentry has given me written permission February 2007 to reissue her book, add pictures and related information.

William Reed has my permission to edit and add pictures to Florence Gentry's book of memories.

Bill has done a lot of work in finding the family past history, and has written books recording the history.

Eugene Gentry

Eugene Gentry

FOND MEMORIES OF MOTHER, FLORENCE GENTRY

By

Eugene Gentry

When I think of Mom, it is like I am a grade school kid. She was the boss of the family, and kept good track of me and brother Paul. She had a police whistle that we could hear half mile away, and when she blew that whistle it meant come home right now.

We lived on four acres on the edge of town, along with a cow and chickens. Mom had a huge garden that she took care of. There were several apple, plum and cherry trees. I remember her in the kitchen with all the jars, stove running full blast, canning the fruits and vegetables.

She plucked and cleaned the chickens for cooking, and skimmed the cream from the milk. It seemed like we had chicken to eat every Sunday, but most likely there was a variety.

She loved music, and played the piano and the violin. About once a month two friends would come to the house and they would play a trio of cello, piano and violin. She also belonged to a women's group and 10 to 12 women would come to the house where they would sew, crochet, knit and visit.

Both mom and dad were very active in the First English Lutheran Church. Every Sunday our family would go to Sunday school at 9:00 AM and church at 11:00 AM, where mom would sing in the choir and dad would usher. Both would help in many other church activities.

Even in later years, mom kept in contact with friends, and after dad died she worked as secretary at the church for many years.

Dad is buried in Billings, Montana, in the military section of the old cemetery on Central Ave and mom is buried across the street in the new cemetery. Many friends came to her funeral.

May they both rest in peace, and I know they are in heaven.

Table of Contents

Those Were The Days
(Golden Memories)

The Home Folks

The many and varied experiences of life from one's recollections are more or less left in the background of the mind as one hurries through life. After the family is raised and one's pace slows down somewhat, the heavy veil, which over all the years holds memories, suddenly becomes thinner and more transparent and as one has time to sit and meditate now and then each dream brings to light a thought of something near and dear to one's heart. Golden memories of what transpired in youth and growing years.

When I was a kid I lived with my Dad,(William H.), Mother (Emily (Olson) one brother,(Stillman A.) older and a sister, (Alice) younger, in a small town in mid Minnesota, called Cokato in Indian language, Meaning "Blue Kittle" or so went the tale of old. Few families lived on our street as it was a short one beginning just a half block to the north of our home, and ending three blocks or so to the south just beyond the high school, and was cut in half by the Great Northern railroad which in those years centered the small towns in Minnesota and North Dakota.

Reed Homestead Cokato
William H. & Emily Reed

REED
William H. and Emily (Olson)
(Married 23 March 1892)

REED
Alice Myrtle Marie's Picture
Stillman (Andre) Andrew Prescott, Elise Lillian Florence
William Henry Ambrose, Emily (Olson)

Our old home was like many other houses in town, a large two story one, taller on one end, grayish in color with trim the same, When it was built way back in the 1880's a stain had been applied to the pine siding for protection but it was never painted. Had it been it would have appeared stately, there on its small knoll overlooking the rest of the grounds, much like a woman seated on a high stool looking over her belonging. But now years later the old house reminded one of a large dried nut. The oil from the original stain was removed long since by the hundreds of summer suns and wintry winds.

Though we kids were ashamed of the ugly looking house it was home, and a good one. And though it was drab the yard was beautiful. Huge oak and elm trees like giant umbrellas had been planted at intervals throughout the yard and mother always had an abundance of lovely flowers throughout the yard from early spring until late fall, and in banks against the house drew one's attention away from the drabness of the house.

Cokato Homestead, 1910

At the time Dad and Mother had brought their first born, a son, into the world Grandmother, (Caroline Koch) who at that time owned the old home, insisted they come and live with her, so an addition was built on, a kitchen with an upstairs bedroom. Grandmother occupied the front part of the house and the upstairs, while our small family lived in the three rooms in the north and east parts of the house, and had the use of an adjoining shed in which coal, wood, and kindling were kept in bins, and extra equipment such as a soft water barrel, the ironing board, tubs, etc., were kept there to be out of the way and still convenient.

When the addition was built the kitchen was four steps lower than the rest of the building. The unusual feature of these steps was that they could be raised up from the right side on hinges, revealing below a nice cool cellar another three steps down, in which mother kept the food needing cooling and the many things she had canned in glass jars and crocks, along with the root vegetables, for winter use.

A cellar in those earlier day us was the only kind of refrigeration at hand until some years later we were thrilled by the purchase of an ice box, which opened at the top for ice. A pantry graced the space to the left of the stairs and that to us youngsters was an intriguing place since most of the time we found goodies waiting for us there.

Below the shed's floor was a large cistern and when it rained mother would let the water that ran from the roof through a drain pipe into the rain barrel placed at the corner of the house and when it was full she would switch the damper in the pipe to let the overflow go into the cistern, which water was drawn into the kitchen by a small pump, a real convenience in those days.

So called hard or drinking water, was plentiful as we had a well with a good sized pump on it near the back door. We kids were well acquainted with the pump handle, a bucket of water for a family of five didn't last long. We never knew who would be called on next to manipulate the handle.

Sometimes we had to add a little water to the upper part of the pump to prime it, in other words to get the water to come up. The barrels of rain water kept on the outside of the house furnished us with plenty of water for other things, as washing clothes, bathing, etc. These barrels were a continual source of interest. When the water had been standing in the barrels for a number of days we would watch the mosquito larva or wrigglers as we called them swimming near the top of the water and we would skim off some of them with our hands. When the barrels were almost empty it was job to wash the sediment free from the sides and bottom of them, rinse them, and place them back under the spouts ready for the next rainfall, a job not looked forward to with very much eagerness.

The matter of taking care of sewage was handled in the manner prevalent in those days. About half way between our house and the barn a well worn path led to the out house, better know as the "back house" which it really was, though it could have been referred to as the little house out back.

During the day the two holer (with a crescent moon cut in the door *see page 115*) tended to our physical needs when nature got demanding. In other words it was our toilet. At the side of the larger holes, intended to fit the adult anatomy, was a lower and smaller one for the young fry. It was also a time before the soft fluffy wiping materials had been invented so good use was made of the old Sears Roebuck catalog. Anyone having to be relieved at night had their choice of two objects called a camber, one a low vessel and one a pail size, usually made of china and on top of which rested a cover with a knitted or crocheted "silencer" around it.

Other things to be disposed of were dishwater,, bathwater, and refuse from the kitchen, Bathwater kept the garden green, dishwater and refuse or so called garbage was placed in a bucket alongside the stove and carried out when full to parts of the garden or if much stuff was in it, it was carried down behind the barn to a sort of compost heap, later dug into the ground. Corn husks and pea hulls which accumulated during the lush season of the summer garden were fed to the horses, and scraps from the table went to the chickens.

To the east and south of our home was a shallow boggy piece of land owned by the canning company (Green Giant) for years, animals grazed on it and over the years and large hummocks had formed. We would take a short cut through the marsh when the weather was dry and would jump from hummock to hummock, a great sport seeing who could land in the middle of them or land in the boggy sections between them.

Even in real dry weather there were sections that were quite spongy but not wet enough to let us down a few inches. Many years later this piece of land was filled in with gravel and dirt so the canning company, which was then in full production, could park their huge corn wagons there. During the summer when we sat on the back stoop and it began to get dark we could see fireflies flitting here and there over the marsh in the cool of evening.

Before proceeding to other things I must tell you we had another outdoor spot called a cyclone cellar This was an underground structure about twenty feet from the house which served us well several times when the summer wind went wild and the lightning and thunder got too sassy for comfort.

Twice a cyclone tried to raze the town it each time swerved first to the north and then to the south of town and did damage only to outlying farms on the east end of town. (In the 80's a storm hit the warehouse of the Green Giant canning company, less than a block from where the homestead stood) Many times when an electrical storm raged the lightning would ring the telephone bells and many time I saw pink light come out from it. No one thought of going near the phone to make a call during one of these storms. Lightning struck often, too, and most people had lightning rods, on top of their houses , sometimes two or three of them. These were connected with a wire which was fastened down to the ground. The lightning would generally follow this wire into the ground and no harm was done, but one in a while the didn't work and a fire resulted.

Our small home was not elaborately furnished. We had good sturdy furniture which withstood the rigors of youth. The floors throught the house were of pine, those in the living room and bed rooms were covered with home-made loom woven rugs, and the kitchen kept almost white by constant weekly scrubbing with strong soap good old Fels Naphtha-plus a good scrub brush and plenty of "elbow grease" Lovely lace curtains hung at the three windows in the living room, behind which were dark green shades that pulled down on a roller. Sometimes they got out of hand when the spring in the wood roller would let loose and the curtain refused to go up or come down. In this case the spring became unwound and mother taught us that if we hung the curtain up full length with one end in the socket and wound it holding one and loose that it would rewind itself, and this it did.

In winter a large coal heater took up goodly space on one side of the living room. Mother was so proud of the fine "furnace" with it chrome trimming, but oh min could it make a hole in the coal bin when the weather really got cold. It was Dad's job until my brother was old enough to hand the hod, then he got the job At night dad would "bank" the fire by putting in plenty of coal, closing the dampers on the stove, Leaving the one in the pipe open so that any fumes might escape. For moisture in the air, a bucket of water was placed on a part of the stove at the back which was flat and when build was made for that purpose. We kids alternated, scrapping about it a good lot of the time as to who was to take out the ashes which accumulated in the large pan beneath the fire grate.

We kids alternated, scrapping about it a good lot of the time as to who was to take out the ashes which accumulated in the large pan beneath the fire grate. But like all kids we did that chore because we knew we had to, squabbling or no.

Another of Dad's jobs was indeed a special procedure before deep winter set in, and which also involved us kids as well as Ma. To begin with Ma had to prod Dad into getting the job done before it got too cold. Dad would buy a few rolls of tar paper and tack it to the house, next we all shoveled manure which had accumulated in the a stack to the side of the barn, into the wheelbarrow and rolled it to the house where it was packed against the house up to the top of the tar paper.

There was lots of straw from old bedding for the horses mixed through the manure so it wasn't so it wasn't too obnoxious so far as smell went but nevertheless a much unwanted job by us kids, about which we had nothing to say or do but help.

Once a year or so mother would rent a rug loom on which she made rag carpets, usually a yard wide and in lengths to fit either the living room or the bed room. The loom had a magic lure and we kids took turns, after having been carefully instructed by mother, working the loom, though of course we tried quickly for the work it entailed didn't match up with our enthusiasm to become masters of the art. The loom had two peddles on it and we would have to work those to change the threads, or warp as it was called, and then run the shuttle, which was like a big wooden needle with an eye on the one end to hold the rags, through the treads and then pull the beater back against the already woven part of the rug. Before the weaving started in earnest mother, who had prepared baskets on baskets of rags from materials given her by neighbors and friends, would invite women to come in for sewing and that was lots of fun. The women would sew rags of color or all white into large balls which were easy to use when the weaving started. Mother was particular that the seams were flat so that there would be no bulges in the rug rows of the finished product. Sometimes she would have to rip the sewing and flatten the seams out. We girls got a good course of instruction in how to do it. Alone with being good help for mother, the "sewing bees" always were well attended because the women knew that when that time of the afternoon came they would be served coffee and a variety of baked goodies to pay them for their work and time spent sewing and visiting.

One event with regard to the rug business was the spring housecleaning when the rugs came up and the bare floors were used during the summer months. Then when fall came and just before school started mother would send out the warming that the rugs would have to be laid, a disaster warning you may be sure.

During the summer mother had ripped the rug apart for easy washing and then sewed it back together again, during her leisure time, and now it was ready for re-laying. It was a tough enough chore taking the carpet up. pulling out all the tacks that held it in place with a special tack hammer, but putting them back in was an even harder job. Our poor fingers and backs howled for mercy before we had finished.

First of all newspapers had to be spread on the bare floor, then new straw from the bedding stack in the barn was put on top of them, flattened out evenly but not too thin so as to keep the cold out, then the rug, centered by mother and with her help and critical eye we went through another do it yourself job. If there was a bunch underneath that we perhaps hadn't smoothed down enough we could use a hat pin, one of those contraptions used by women in those days to keep their hats on, and perchance for a weapon if needed, and we could reach under the rug with it and flatten out the bulge. Finally when this work of art was over we were proud of the "new look" and the rug was nice and clean.

Another fall chore was helping to dig up and than pick up the root vegetables potatoes, beets, carrots, and get them to the cellar for winter use. Turnips and rutabagas were also harvested along with the cabbages, corn that had dried on the stalks for chicken feed later on.

The last fall chore was getting the big heater from the lean to shed into the living room, but this eventually was accomplished after much grunting, sweating and some cussing. on the part of Dad and the fellow helping him.

REED
Emily (Olson) and William Henry Ambrose
Stillman Obadiah and Caroline Mary (Koch)

Now from Home Folks to Relatives

As mentioned in the first part of this episode we lived with my Dad's mother, Grandma Reed nee Caroline Mary Koch. Grandpa Reed, (Stillman (Obadiah), for whom my brother was named) was a New Hampshirian but he had died the same year my brother was born and before my folks moved to Grandmas, but Great Grandpa John Koch, her father lived with her until I was six years old.

I can well remember that many times I sat on the old man's knee and fondled his beautiful white beard, and how he did love us little kids.

He was 92 when he died and I can still see him as he laid in his coffin in the upper bedroom. There were no mortuaries in those days so the deceased was kept in the home until time for burial.

Grandma Caroline Reed was a real character. She came from good old Pennsylvania Dutch stock. Through her childhood she had been considered 'Puny" but she was married at the age of 15. Grandpa had served as a soldier in the Civil War and was a congenial person so Grandma told me in later years. He had established a dray business and was kept busy hauling all kinds of materials and equipment. For salesmen, merchants and others needing things moved. When grandpa died, my Dad took over the business.

KOCH FAMILY
Caroline, John, Aunt May (Engler)
Cousin Emma (Engler) ?
Baby Gladys (?)

To Grandma (Caroline) and Grandpa (Stillman O.) five children were born, Three of whom survived; my Dad and his two older sisters, Mary & Emma. Grandmother's folks lived mostly in the Chaska and Jordan areas of Minnesota, some 30 miles or so south of Minneapolis, where they farmed. Mary was about 18 years older than my father and had to watch over the other two, Emma and William. As Grandma did all the family sewing which was a goodly bit those days what with the numerous petticoats the girls had to wear not to mention the other underclothes, the men's and boy's shirts, and her own garments. But she was a good seamstress. Many times I watched her piecing together tiny lengths of thread or yarn thinking" why doesn't she just throw them away" but the standard word at all times was "save" and everyone did just that. A part of her sewing equipment was mighty intriguing to we two granddaughters. It was a box containing lengths of ribbon, lace beading, fancy braids, etc. Some times she would condescend to give us a trifling piece or two to add to our doll "rags" collection.

Elsie Lillian Florence (Reed) Gentry
donated this quilt to the Cokato History Museum

Diana R.(Koch) and Michael Engler 1855

Grandmother was not dubbed a religious woman. I can't recall her going to church but I am sure she did. It seems in a vague sort of way that she was Presbyterian. However, she read her bible regularly and could carry on an intelligent discussion about its contents with others and was well read on current events. (She was the first woman to vote in Cokato, which was noted in the Enterprise Newspaper).

The poor dear was the victim of the affliction called asthma and suffered with it many long years. In her later years I once visited her and noted she didn't wheeze any more so I Said "Grandma, you don't have asthma any more" and she smiled and said "no, I finally wore it out"

Grandmother made many trips in her early days to Minneapolis and always invested small sums of money on trivial gifts for her grand kids. This was a most pleasant time for us and we waited breathlessly to see what she had brought us, when she returned

At home an invitation to have a meal with her would come at intervals, when it was convenient for her, to my sister or I and once in a while to the both of us a the same time. Perhaps it was easier to get the full attention when only one was there. She never lectured us that I recall. Our reprimands came via the front door when we did things we shouldn't have done. I can still hear "Shut that gate"! Whether we kids were going out or coming in it was always the same admonition. Some of the time we didn't even make it through the gate far enough to get it closed.

Grandmother (Caroline) was death on any dog that seemed inclined to wander in the direction of the house, so she insisted that the gate be closed, why, we could never understand or one could throw a half dozen of them through any section of the fence without much difficulty. Her front door was immediately opposite the ill regarded gate and a time we wondered if she had eyes in the back of her head or if she was spying on us all the time, though I am sure that thought was a fit far-fetched for she had plenty of work to keep her busy at all hours of the day.

To get away from family chores after the children were big enough to take care of themselves Grandma would board the local train and head for Minneapolis or Chaska where her sister (Diana) lived a matter of 30 miles or so from the city. Our small family would some times be invited to go with her.

My great Uncle Michael and Aunt Diana (Engler) lived on a farm and the homestead laid between a hill and a slope of farm land. We would go up to the top of the hill along with our cousins' kids and we would run down the hill, level off at the house and start down the slope. One had to be real agile to jump the small creek that footed the slope or get a ducking and perhaps a licking on top of it..

Dinner at this farm home was something to remember even on non-celebration days. The table literally groaned as did we for having to wait until the elders had finished their meal, no firsts for the small fry those days. We didn't mind too much, though as there was always ample food left for us even if it wasn't as appetizingly arranged as for the first indulgence. We always enjoyed our visit as there were so many things to see and do.

My Aunt, Mary Caroline, was the eldest of the five children, 18 years older than my father who was the youngest. Charley and Alice died in early youth. Aunt Emma next old than Dad loved him very much, and we always thought Aunt Emma was tops. Aunt Mary had to take charge of the family much of the time when she was old enough to realize her responsibilities, as Grandma then was busy nursing sick folks in the circle of friend and neighbors, also acting a mid-wife a times. She was called on many times since the Doctor lived miles away. She also spent extra time selling extracts to make a little pin money as she received small pay for her nursing duties.

Mary was a good cook and with the help of Emma managed the youngest, my father, who dealt them plenty of misery and caused concern at time. Aunt Mary told me about the time Dad had Scarlet fever. In those days the food for patients with scarlet fever was mighty slim. Grandma had dried apples earlier in the fall and stored them in one of the upper rooms. In an unguarded moment my father, sick as he was supposed to be, snitched a goodly amount of the forbidden apples and proceeded to eat them. By medical standards then he should have died, but apparently they didn't even make him sicker. When asked why he took the apples he said "Well, I'm Starving to death".

Another time Aunt Mary was delegated to take my brother up to the loft to bed. They had to climb a short ladder in the process as the stairs hadn't been built up to then. Aunt Mary followed behind Dad with a candle and he turned and said "don't get so close or you'll burn my hind end" but he used a word always conferred on a donkey. When they got into the loft Aunty shook him up a bit and that didn't help the language any.

TAYLOR
Maude Alice (Golladay), Mary Caroline (Reed)
Harry J.E., Mildred Jessie, Edward G

When she was 17 Aunt Mary married a new comer to the small town, a fellow by the name of Edward Taylor, Born in (London) England.

How he happened to come to Cokato remains a mystery and what his calling or occupation so called was, no one ever seemed to figure out but he did many things a so called Jack of all Trades. We kids always held him in awe for he would tell us some far-fetched tales and could keep us entertained for hours had we stayed that long. Every bit of his vividly portrayed years brought characters and places into real life for us, and he delighted in telling them. Most of his tales would rival in interest with Gulliver's Travels or better. He fought the battle of Shiloh (Civil War) many a time, was "shot through like a sieve" to hear him tell it, and told us he put a rag on the ramrod of his gun and cleaned out his wounds. Sounded incredible. He told us too of other Civil War Experiences through I doubt if he was more than a water boy or bugler since he was very young at the time.

After Ed and Mary's marriage they built a nice home in the center of town. It was well planned, with a large living room with a bay window to the street (a joy to Grandma Reed in later years as she could watch all the goings on down the street), a small bedroom, a large dining room and kitchen together, a summer kitchen into which the stove was moved along with the table and cupboards.

When spring arrived; a pantry that was always the center of attraction to us kids. Upstairs was entered by a carpeted stair where there were two bed rooms, one large one a smaller one, a large attic and a hall .The attic under the eaves required the "bends" to explore it contents. The yard was a thing of beauty since Uncle Ed was a gardener along with his other talents. Back of the house he always planted a bi garden and I shall never forget the beautiful sweet peas he raised each year. They grew taller than our heads and were lush with blossoms. He always planted them in rows going north and south and used a wire fence for them to "vine" on. Their neighbor said of Uncle that he could plant a broomstick and it would produce.

I don't recall what he did for bugs except knocking the potato bugs off with a stick into a can of Paris green (poison). I am sure he didn't have many others for there were all kinds of birds to take care of that, and they did also help themselves to his strawberries and tomatoes as they ripened. His one pest was chickens which belonged to the occupants of the city's larger hotel which adjoined the Taylor property.

I distinctly remember what happened one day journey when I dropped by to see the folks on my (out of the way) home from school. One of the chickens from the hotel yard had wandered over to pick a few tidbits from Uncle's lettuce and tomatoes. Uncle had been using a three corned file to sharpen a small hoe, and suddenly said "think I'll have me some chicken for a good stew tomorrow. He aimed the file at the chicken and pinned it's neck to the ground, went over, rung it neck and proceeded to prepare it for the morrow's meal.

Uncle's stories were not the only attraction for us kids. He was an excellent cook, and it wasn't long until Aunt Mary took advantage of this fact and he finally did all of the meal preparation. He loved to stir up a batch of raised doughnuts, or a roly-poly made from bread dough and filled with apples, served with lemon sauce. In the winter he made varieties of pies.

Many times the folks would take us down to visit in the evening and before it got too late Uncle Ed. Would disappear for a little while then came back in with a huge bread pan filled with pop corn, dripping with butter and well salted. Boy how we loved that. We would all sit around the dining table with its lovely red shaded lamp-shade pulled down over the center.

Raising horseradish was a side issue of the garden in business for Uncle. When ready he would dig, wash, and scrape the roots and spend many hours grinding it and shedding many tears during the process. Sometimes he would have a wooden tubful of the ground "tongue stingers" and many times we kids got in on the grinding and crying, and oh boy it did sting our eyes. Uncle would then mix the stuff with white vinegar (the dark vinegar had a tendency to darken the horseradish and it wasn't attractive for selling), then he would bottle it and sell it to the towns people.

Uncle Ed and Aunt Mary owned a small cabin on Point Lake, out of Willmar, Minnesota a town about 50 miles west of Cokato, (Near Eagle Lake between Willmar and Spicer), and Uncle spent a lot of time there during the summer. One time when my brother was quite young he visited Uncle Ed, going up to Willmar on the train where Uncle Ed met him. How they got to the lake is a moot question but likely they walked. Stillman wanted to fish so uncle made a raft, putting a couple of boxes on it for the young fisherman to sit on and the other to hold the fish. Then he tied the raft, equipped with a long rope, to a tree stump. Stillman would paddle out the length of the rope and sit and fish to his hearts content. Betimes Uncle spent some of the time "horse trading" and he could sell almost anything. Sometimes people got the worst of the bargain because they didn't understand his tactics. One time he had an old stove he wanted to sell. An interested fellow

COFIELD
Lorenzo and Emma Louise (Reed)

asked him how much he wanted for it. "$10" said Ed. "How much will you give me"? The fellow got mad and left. Had he dickered he could have bought it for 50 cents.

Aunt Mary was a quiet sort, and at one time was badly afflicted with eczema on her hands so she was might glad to turn over the cooking to her good husband, along with anything that required using her hands in water so poor Ed was burdened with the washing to clothes as well as that of dishes. However their two youngsters were soon old enough to help. Henry, the older of the two and Emma named for her aunt. They were grown before we kids came to town so to speak. They were more like Aunt and Uncle than cousins to us.

My Uncle Lorenzo, or Ren as he was called, married my Dad's younger sister Emma. His name was Cofield. The built a lovely brick home in Annandale, a town about 18 miles north of Cokato. How we loved to visit them in their lovely big house. Uncle Ren was in the cement business and later became a banker in the small bank there. We thought he was somebody when one day

Cofields' REO touring car

he drove over from Annandale in a brand new Reo. He was the first one in the family to own a car, and I shall never forget the thrill of seeing it for the first time, and being allowed to get into it for further inspection.

It was like a old fashioned buggy; large wheels with the body of the car 'setting high". A two seater with shiny black upholstery. When driving uncle wore an Ulster (a long loose overcoat) and a tight fitting cap with a visor while Aunty had a light weight coat and a big hat with a scarf tied over it to hold it on during the driving for even a 20 or 25 miles and hour there was a certain amount of breeze created. How proud we kids were to climb into it and ride that wonderful piece of machinery.

A special attraction, for me at least, was Aunt Emma's baby grand piano and I, being musical, wanted so badly to at least touch it but did await Auntie's approval, which she did give at intervals. The parlor which housed it was an "off limits" place most of the time except when guests were invited to partake of their hospitality. However, a large dining and living room (now called family rooms), and a huge kitchen sufficed for kids, play and eating.

The prize of that family was their faithful maid who lived with them for many years and we all loved her so much. Her name was Anna Oletsky I can still see her hustling around getting a huge meal and setting the table properly for company with all the lovely china, crystal and linen, and without the least bit of consternation. She was a gem and we enjoyed her presence.

The folks always took her with them when they visited us , She married late in life but then lived in Cokato as both Uncle Ren and Aunty Emma had died. Even after I was grown I enjoyed visiting with her. The folks (Cofields) had raised three sons who all married and left home while we youngsters were quite young.

Since my Dad was the youngest of the three I have left writing about him until last and since I have already told you about his early life I will start when he took over the dray business after his father died. He was about 29 at the time, though he had worked on the dray for a number of years before that so knew the ins and outs of the business. He spent much time at the depot meeting trains and incoming salesmen, whose trunks and sample cases he took to one or the other of the hotels in town indicated as preference by the salesmen. Neither of the hotels were far from the depot a block or so perhaps but too far to carry a trunk or heavy case. Dad would also do odd jobs of hauling for the several merchants in town who wanted goods shipped to other towns or who had stuff coming in on the freights. Dad had a good sized dray wagon and two nice horses, one a grey, called Fred and the other a roan, called Frank.

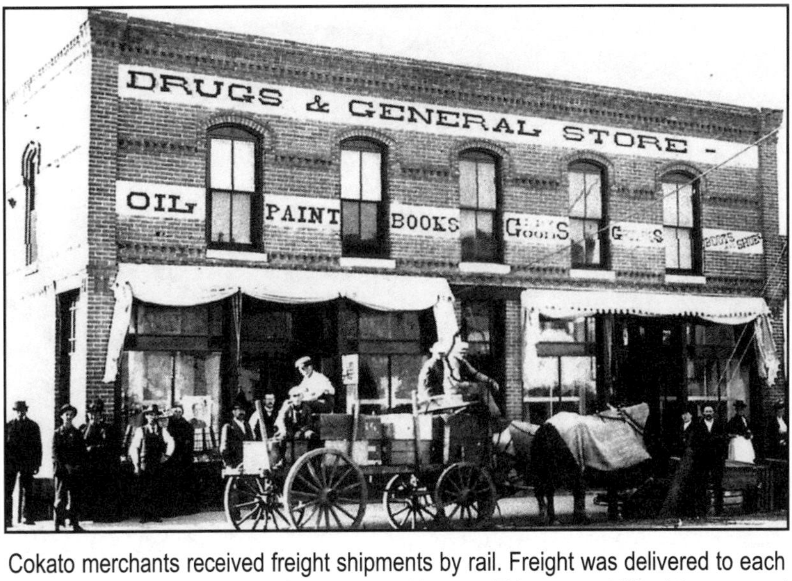

Cokato merchants received freight shipments by rail. Freight was delivered to each store by the "dray line," drawn by a team of horses. This scene, Millard Avenue and Third Street, shows the "Thelander building," about 1904.

We youngsters did love those horses and they us. When we were old enough to look after ourselves we would run to meet dad and the dray when he came home for his meals and would get onto the dray or on one of the horses' backs and ride in like kings on chargers.

One time in the fall mother had dug up a large number of carrots and put them in the wheelbarrow to dry before storing them in the cellar. It happened she had left it at the edge of the barn where it was shady yet warm enough to dry the carrots. Old Fred spotted them and instead of going directly into the bar as he usually did he made a circle to the wheelbarrow and helped himself to a good sized mouthful of the carrots. You could almost see the mischief in his eyes as he snitched them.

William H. Reed on left & a hired man
The horses Frank and Fred

One thing connected with the horses is a barn loft full of hay, and intriguing place for growing youngsters. We had many good bottom warmers on that hay from the very top of the loft and on down. Sometimes we would go down the opposite direction and land in on of the mangers to the surprise of the horse or cow who happened to be there at the time, and who viewed the cause of interruption of their feeding time.

Our cow, a jersey, at one time reduced the size of the hay in the mow and how we hated that cow, not that she wasn't gentle, but because we had to lug her milk around to grandmother and to some other people the folks knew. Of course we enjoyed the milk she gave and the cream and butter, but the chores she added to our day wasn't in the least appreciate.

At a busy time of the year in the dray business Dad would hire a man to help him. He always treated as a member of the family. I remember one fellow in particular as he was a persistent tease and was always picking on my sister Alice and I. One time we girls got all dressed up in some of mothers cast offs and thought we were high class as we paraded in front of the men to show off as they were drinking their afternoon coffee. "All you need now is a beau" said the hired man and I innocently put my hand to my head and said "I haven't any room for a bow where will I put it"? He and Dad had a hearty laugh. Dad was always kind hearted sort of easy going, sometimes to mother consternation, especially when she wanted him to do something or get around and collect his bills. He didn't live as long as his sisters, leaving for better places when he was 72.

Mother was 19 when she got married and came from Swedish parents who arrived in America in the mid 1860's from Malmo, Sweden a place close to Stockholm shortly after mother's oldest sister was born. The settled in the area southwest of Cokato on a farm about two miles from a little hamlet called Stockholm by previous settlers from Sweden. Grand Dad Andrew did many things besides farming, of which I will recite later. Emily, my mother, was second in line, Carrie, Mathilda, and Altin being the rest of the brood.

Like all the other girls in those days they (Mother and Annie) were pushed out of the nest when it was felt they could do something on their own and usually would go to St. Paul where they did household duties for wealthy families in the cities. So when mother got married she was well equipped in the art of cooking, sewing and general house work, as well as love for her hubby and the three children she bore. We were all blessed with three prefixes to our father's name. I was Elsie Lillian Florence, My sister Alice Myrtle, Marie and my brother Stillman (after his paternal grandfather, Andrew Prescott. At times my brother would gladly have shed the Prescott for he was nicknamed "Biscuit" by the teaming hoard of restless, active boys in that small town. They were not bad boys, just rowdy and full of the Old Nick. Since it had become a fad to attach a nickname to every boy in the town Stillman was rebaptized "Biscuit" which name stuck to him all his life.

As we grew older I called him that many times, more in love than anything else. It just seemed to be part of him. Some of the other nicknames were 'Big Cork, Little Cork (brothers) , Knobbin, Satchel, Bust Ole (his fathers name Mabusth) Pete and Repeat who were twins, Sweden, Bull, Luggins, Skaning, Spike, Henkicker, Piecrust, Bone, and Moss. I often wondered why the didn't get around to nickname the girls.

Mother was raised a strict Lutheran and saw to it that we went to Sunday School fairly regular. The Lutheran Church was build at the far end of town to the southeast while we lived in the northwest section with the railway in between to mother sent us to the Baptist Church, only a few blocks from home, for our basic training. Another reason was that she decided we should learn our Sunday School lessons in English and a the Lutheran Church only Swedish was taught. We didn't mind as we loved our teacher and the cards she gave us each Sunday.

Edith Olson 1920

Later years Dad had acquired a huge picture frame from on of the city merchants and mother filled it full of our Sunday School Cards. We kids were so proud of that picture. It hung on the bedroom wall for many years and I have wondered time and again up to this writing what ever happened to the huge picture. As we grew into preteens we would go to the church on Sunday evenings to the revivals and I can well remember how we would sit in the very back seats and giggle over the goings on. Small wonder we weren't asked to leave by the ushers but maybe they felt we might finally take an interest in the sermon at least.

When I reached confirmation age I went to "read" for the Episcopal ministers, Dr Erickson, along with my cousin Edith (Olson), whose mother died when she was only 12 and she was brought up by a fine Episcopalian family, they too were Swedish. I being much the same in beliefs as the Lutherans, mother felt it didn't matter too much, and so I went through a year's study before confirmation. There were four of us two girls and two boys, and one of the boys later took training and became a minister.

Mother's parents, as I mentioned before came to America from Sweden. I was always in love with grandmother's name (Pernilla) and wished that my folks had at least given me it for a middle name.

Grandfather Olson's' name was Andrew (Olaf). A stern looking gentleman with a beard, but though stern looking and so called straight laced, he was a kindly sort of person too. He raised his family well, though not richly. Mother's older brother Olaf died as an infant and sister Anna were born in Sweden but her three sisters and a brother were born in this county. Aunt Carrie (Caroline) died when she was about 20, Aunt Mathilda Eunice, more familiarly know to us kids as Aunt Tillie, died when she was 33, who was my cousin Edith's mother, and Uncle Altin Olaf, the youngest of the brood. Aunt Anna lived to be over ninety as did mother, and Uncle Altin was in the upper 80's at the time of his demise.

The following is an account my mother sent me of the things Grandmother did: "Back in the early1880's Grandmother raised flax, then prepared it for spinning thread, later woven into towels on a small loom.

When the flax was ready she would thresh it by beating it with a large wooden knife, much like a machete only all wood with one edge thinned like a dull knife edge. She would beat it until the straw was beaten to a pulp and brushed away the she would gather the precious flax and do the spinning later, weaving it then as she had time.

OLSON
Andrew Olaf and Pernilla (Olson)

Anna (Olson) Anderson

Grandmother (Pernilla) Olson was also a bookbinder, bringing the necessary equipment with her from Sweden. This consisted of one large oak press and a smaller one a contraption which contained a knife which could be adjusted to trim the edges of the paper or the books pages. After a book was patched, if necessary and rebound she would put it on one of the presses, according to the size of the book, and then trim it. A neighbor would get the

ANDERSON FAMILY

Photo (ca 1891)

John Peter Anderson Married Brita Nelson 4 Feb 1876 Five Children were born to this union. Ester died at birth Left to right Hulda, Laura, Albert, Amanda

Anna Olson Married John Peter Anderson 7 Nov 1889 The child on Anna's lap is Ester. Six Children were born to this union. Not shown Selma, Edna, Louise, Edwin, Clarence

necessary white paper for fly leaves and the leather for the back of the books was purchased by mail from a publishing house in St. Paul, Minnesota, as were the mottled covers for the books. The price for Grandmother's work was done more for love than for remuneration for she realized how much the precious books meant to her friends and neighbors and how glad the old-timers were to get their books mended and rebound, most of which the had brought from Sweden.

Emily Reed (Olson)

Both Grandmother (Pernilla) and Grandfather (Andrew Olson)) were devout church members and lived their lives accordingly. Sunday was a day of quietness, after an hour or more in church, and as few duties as possible were done. They too, were musical. Grandpa (Andrew) was a cantor in the church a Stockholm. I still have a psalm a book he used. It is divided through the center horizontally, with the words below and music above, this for the purpose of using different tunes with the many songs if need be.

When Grandmother (Pernilla) Olson, as well as other older ladies, and even some of the younger ones, would go to church the would put a sprig of tansy and a couple of leaves of Sweet Mary with their handkerchiefs and placed them between the leaves of their psalm books and off to church they would go. In church they would take a sniff of the home made "perfume" I remember well how Grandma (Pernilla) used to tie a black kerchief over her had for church taking it off before entering. In winter the scarf went on first and the hat on top.

Grandpa (Andrew) was a tailor and made many a suit for men and boys. He was surely a versatile person. He also taught school at one time. I still have a quaint quart crock bottle which held the extra supply of ink, and also a small individual desk ink well, that fit in a hole in the desk and which was filled from the larger bottle.

On the small piece of land the folks owned Grandpa (Andrew) raised a cow, a few pigs and grain for the animals. The cow grazed during the summer and supply of hay sufficed for the winter months. A big garden was managed by Grandma (Pernilla). She always had a pattern for the garden and for her flower beds. At the far end of the garden was a grape arbor, in front of which was a bed of tansy (a bitter aromatic plant with small yellow flowers) and Sweet Mary.

A path from the house lead to this area. On either side of the path were also the vegetable beds and these were backed by currant and lilac bushes. Apple trees had been planted here and there though the yard. When fall came Grandma (Pernilla) was busy with jelly making from the grapes and apples along with apple sauce, apple butter, dried apples , etc.

The distance from our home to Grandpa (Olson's) farm was about three miles but we gladly trudged the distance at frequent intervals during the summer, resting beneath a huge elm that provided welcome shade, about half ways there. This tree was lovingly dubbed "the resting tree". Many times we would take our shoes off, or if barefooted rub our weary feet. Sometimes a kindly farmer would come along in a wagon and offer us a ride.

We always looked forward to a treat when we arrived, generally in the form of a pan of fresh milk with thick cream on top from the cooler, which Grandma (Pernilla) would set out for us. We would dip slices of her homemade bread in the cream, turn it over on a small plate, eat it and then drink the milk. After our tummies were filled and our visit with Grandma (Pernilla) and Grandpa (Andrew) if he was there, they talking Swede and we English with both understanding the other, we would go to the high clay bank alongside the house and dig up a few shovalsful of clay which we molded into anything we happened to think of after the water had been added to it. When we tired of that we would to the barn area and pig pen and tease the pigs. How much fun it was to get them grunting and squealing.

Then we would finally wind up taking a walk through the lovely woods to the north of the place on adventuresome trips, imagining all sort of things, finally when that got boring we would start for home, tired but happy kids, arriving in time for the call to a nice warm supper.

After Grandfather (Andrew) died Grandma (Pernilla) moved into a small three room apartment across from the schoolhouse, Many times we kids would run over during recess and get a snack. She always loved to have us come although it was not a daily visit..orders from our folks.

Later Grandma (Pernilla) moved to our home, but she was so quiet all the time one hardly knew she was there. Among her belongs was a lovely light oak organ, which she taught me to play. Many a time early evening she would sit on the bench and play quietly, the hymns she loved so much. I shall never forget when she passed to her glory. It was in February (1920) and cold with much snow on the ground, Her casket had to be placed on a bob sled as no hearse could make it through the deep snow and we rode in another sled behind it. It was four miles to the cemetery of the church in Stockholm to which she belonged, where she was buried alongside grandpa. We missed the dear soul for a long time.

Chapter on Early Entertainment

Commercial entertainment was unknown. We did have an Edison Phonograph with a so called "Morning Glory" horn, as it was shaped just like a morning glory flower, hence the name. This transferred the music and voice from a cylinder by a diamond point on the end of the horn from the cylinder into the horn. By the time radio came into the homes we had accumulated quite a number of cylinders.

After they had been on the market for quite a while Dad (William H. Reed) bought an ear phone crystal radio. It wasn't made of glass but that was the name given them. We had to take turns listening, and the programs were generally good. Before these modes of entertainment were in general use there was the photograph albums, the stereoscope, a two sectioned magnifying glass on top of a bracket and a handle below to hold it by to view the pictures placed in the rack in front of the glass. This so called entertainer graced the living room center table along with the albums.

Of course we youngsters, along with others in the neighborhood, played all the then known kid games: hop scotch, tag, rope jumping, cracking the whip, baseball, croquet, swimming in the summer and in the winter skating and bob-sledding.

The elders played cards, Whist or 500, since bridge as it is know today had not been invented, though some form no doubt was played by the aristocrats. The also enjoyed a game of croquet, went to church socials accompanied by the young fry; sewing and kaffee klatches, mostly for the women; and the annual spelling bees celebrated at the local school.

Movies finally arrived in town, and everyone enjoyed the slapstick and silent drama of those days.

Once a year the County (Wright) Fair was the main attraction. This was held on the town streets with booths set up for all sorts of exhibits. The women all vied for First

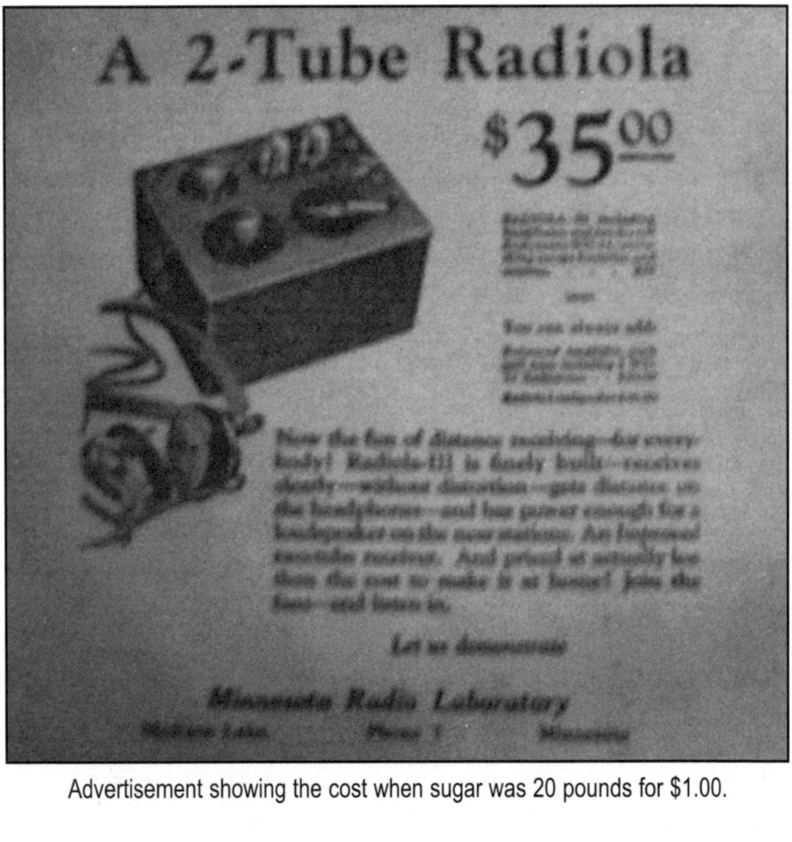

Advertisement showing the cost when sugar was 20 pounds for $1.00.

A two Tube Radiola (ca 1920's)
The radio is still in the family

prizes on their pies, cakes, cookies, jams, jellies and vegetables. They also brought knitted articles, sewing, crocheted items and quilts on which their hopes were pinned for the coveted prizes, which in those days didn't amount to a great deal of monetarily but the honor meant a lot to them.

The special space occupied by the carnival was the drawing card for the children. The merry-go-round the main attraction. The fair lasted a week and people from all over the county attended as we as participated. Races of all sorts were a part of the program too.

After supper entertainment for the men between times was a visit with friends over the bar of the local saloon which sometimes ended in reprimands from the ladies whose husbands showed up at home later a bit inebriated.

Another phase of entertainment was dancing. Brother, the oldsters and the youngsters enjoyed that. Every now and then one of the lodges would sponsor a big dance with a lunch at midnight. The masons and modern

Woodmen were active organizations in those days and they loved to get together for a social. Dances were held in a big hall on the second floor o a building owned by the Mabusth brothers, clothiers or habasherers and a small fee was paid to them for the use of the hall. Many times the sponsors would ask my mother and a local fiddler, Mr. Pickruhn, to do the playing for the dances and dad to call the dances when a quadrille was asked for. I always loved dancing perhaps because when we kids were still very small mother and dad would take us to the hall with them, well bundled, and we slept away to the rhythm of the music.

Stereoscope 1900

Whether that was the reason or the fact that I was born feet first is a moot question as to whether that had anything to do with the love for the art. All through my life the minute I heard quick music I was ready to dance. As we grew up we still would go with the folks the dance hall in those das was a respectable place and everyone except the straight laced church people attended. Their kids went to the small outlaying towns to dance and cut up on the sly, for Pa and Ma knew their kids were above any need for censorship and of course there was dancing was for young and old of a Saturday night out in some farmers big barn hay loft, a good old hoedown (square dance) with loads of fun and food before and afterwards.

I remember one time when we went to a dance in a hayloft that had been cleaned ready for a new crop of hay, and though it was perfectly safe the floor seemed to buckle and sway, and we were almost afraid to dance on it.. These dances always ended up in the wee small hours but it was clean fun and there was no liquor, hence no fights and no hangovers.

A movie house was finally built and everyone enjoyed the slapstick and silent drama movies of those days.

We kids had many escapades. One was jumping on the wheat wagons in the fall, riding them into the elevator ramp and then riding the empties down the opposite side of the loading bins. Most of the drivers knew us and would slow the horses down so we could conveniently jump off, we would visit with old John O'Jampers, a tall robust Finn who owned the elevator and had an office on one side of it. We liked him and he always seemed glad to see us, perhaps because it was a lonely job. He warned us to be careful but never threatened us.

Between times the trucks and would drop a lot of wheat while unloading and John would get us to sweep it up for mother's chickens. That way he got work done that he would have had to do and we go the feed for the chickens. He also taught us to speak Finn as did the Finnish kids who lived next door to us. It was a lingo that was hard to master but along with the everyday words, and howdys and goodbyes, we go along just fine. One phrase I still remember was "ala moola sirap laipa" which was asking for a piece of bread with molasses on it.

In winter time there were plenty of bob sleds to hop on for a ride a block or two, then we would catch another going in the opposite direction Dad and Mother didn't approve of this but they likely figured we would get tired of it like everything else. Sometimes the drivers would crack their whips in our direction for they too sensed the danger, when we would jump off they would wave the whips as mush as to say" have fun, I wouldn't have hit you anyway"

Skating was of prime interest to the young fry during the winter months but we were never allowed on the lake until the "ice" man, who later cut ice from it for household use, said it was safe to skate on. The lake, called Brooks Lake, was about a half mile from our home. It was a mile long and a half mile wide and offered plenty of room for everyone who wanted to enjoy the art of gliding along on a pair of steel runners. A bonfire in the evening helped keep the skaters warm. My skating career ended when my skate ran into a crack in the ice, sending me through the air and ending up with a battered anatomy. The sport sort of lost it glamour for me.

In the summer families took advantage of the lakes beautiful shore line and had picnics, get togethers and of course fishing for the men and boys out in their boats.

The lake was well stocked with fish and they would bring in bass, sunfish and croppies to be pan fried at these outings. And there was plenty of swimming for anyone interested in that sport.

In winter too it was a sight to see small huts set up by the fishermen for protection from the cold and wind so they could conveniently and comfortably fish through the ice. They would cut a hole a foot or so wide through the ice and then hopefully catch some of them on their hooks. My Dad William (Will) and Brother Stillman did a lot of fishing in the summer but none in the cold weather.

On the northeast edge of the lake was a large building which was owned by the ice company, for in those days there were no automatic refrigerators and if one was lucky to own a regular so called ice box, it was fed with a huge chunk of ice in it upper area, zinc lined with a hole in the bottom and a pipe running to a basin beneath the ice box to catch the water fro the melting ice. This was a chore we girls got, that of emptying the basin each day (which we of course sometimes forgot) and had to mop up the water from the floor, along with mother's admonitions.

The Folks would order ice as they needed it and the ice man would deliver, it coming in with a huge pair of picers hooked into the ice and flung over his shoulder. Many times he would be carrying a hundred pound piece.

When the lake was frozen to the depth of two feet the crews would start sawing it out, much like one would saw logs, and would drag them up to the big warehouse like building, built for ice storage, on sleds where it was packed between thick layers of sawdust. We kids spent many hours watching the cutting and storing of these big chunks, shivering away but not having sense enough to get going on our way home.

Trains

Another one of the delights of our childhood was watching the trains come and go. In those early days we had two so called "locals" passenger trains for the accommodation of those wishing to go somewhere, and two fast trains what carried mail, that didn't stop. Boy how those trains went through town, constantly whistling and streaking past like a bolt of lighting. They actually moaned and you could hear them for miles both coming and going. Freight trains too were frequent. Silk, coming from Japan was carried on what were know as "silk trains" and they sure whizzed through our village to eastern manufacturers as not too much time could be taken in the delivery of a fragile cargo.

Then the slower freight trains with 30 to 50 cars at the very most that stopped to unload wares ordered by the merchants. When my brother (Stillman) was in his late teens he applied for a job as a brakeman on one of the short runs from St. Paul to Willmar, about 100 miles, he got it. I heard him say in later years that he gave all the credit of being a good brakeman to the engineer he worked under,, who was kind, patient and must have thought a good deal of the young fellow he had to teach. The man in charge of the string of freight cars was called a freight conductor, and was in charge of the cargo in each car.

He had to know which cars had to be set out on the side track in each town. This was called "spotting". The several brakies on the train and the engineer really knew how to cut those cars from the train and get them on the side track for unloading, a work of art in the eyes of us kids. Many years later my brother (Stillman) had reached the rank of freight conductor, and then a passenger conductor on the Empire Builder.

When the spotting of the cars for Cokato was finished he would climb onto the rear of the caboose and as they passed the final crossing, just a short distance from mother (Emily's) home he would blow the air whistle as a signal to Mother (Emily) that he was on that run. She was always on the alert when a freight pulled into town. At intervals when there was a long wait for right-of-way for other trains Stillman would dash home for a cup of coffee and a chat with Mother (Emily).

The men on the train crew held forth in the little red house on the end of the train.

When railroad men referred to the crummy, hack or parlor car they were referring to the caboose, the little red house. They had bunks to rest on and a stove for warmth in winter, the top of which held a water bucket and a coffee pot. I recall my brother (Stillman) saying "most of the time you could float a horseshoe in the coffee" it was so strong. In the small cuplolo on the top of the caboose the men could watch the scenery go by or check (hot boxes) bums riding on top of the cars, a common thing then.

The train crews spent much time waiting on the sidetracks for orders from the dispatcher in St. Paul or Willmar as to their next move. The orders were relayed to them by the local depot agent (telegrapher). (Stillman learned the Morse code while hanging around the depot in his spare time).

The East bound local passenger train arrived around four o'clock in the afternoon and set the pace for the 4 p.m. kaffee klatches around the town. It was also the time of arrival of us kids from school and we usually found fresh bread or cookies awaiting us.

A ride on one of the locals was an unusual treat for youngsters those days. Minneapolis was a place we visited most of the time and it was 50 miles away, or to Chaska a short ride on another branch out of Minneapolis called the St. Louis, to where Grandma (Caroline)Reed's sister (Diana nee Koch Engler) lived. We didn't mind the green velour seats, straight as a board with no adjustments for comfort, nor did we mid the dirt and cinders from the engine coming in the windows when they were open. The conductor, much of the time an older man, always congenial, though once in a while some sober faced gent would take over or a young fellow being broke in who thought he knew it all.

The delight to us kids was the fellow who came through the coaches burdened down with baskets of candy, fruit or sandwiches which he was peddling (No diners then at least for the coach passengers) so naturally we had a part in helping him dispose of his wares even though the ride took only a little over an hour.

As the passenger train started it journey the conductor came through the cars and collected the tickets, some of which were worn in the bands of the men's hats no doubt they thought it would be easier access for the conductor and they wouldn't have to be digging in their pockets for it.

The noon train arrives from the east, 1905-10. At that time Cokato was served by four passenger trains daily, two west-bound, two east-bound.

In the earliest years the conductor signed his cars in pencil, and at the end of the run they were returned to the railroad official in charge of these tickets. Later a conductor on of the eastern lines came up with the idea of using punches to identify each conductor since a pencil marks could be easily erased and the tickets used again, which they were this causing much lost to the railroad company., No two punch marks were alike and each conductors punch was registered. If any discrepancies occurred the conductor was immediately identified.

Did you know that trains have a language all their own, via the whistle? Train whistles are never blown "Just for fun". Every time a locomotive engineer blows his whistle he is saying something important. Having a father (William) and brother (Stillman) on the railroad it was fun to try to interpret the whistles when we heard them. The most common of signals is two long, a short and a long, reminding pedestrians and vehicles "I am approaching the grade crossing, wait, let me by. This we well knew was the flyer or silk train. One short toot means the train is stopping, two shorts is always an answer to any signal

Cabose built to scale by Stillman A. Reed 1960's

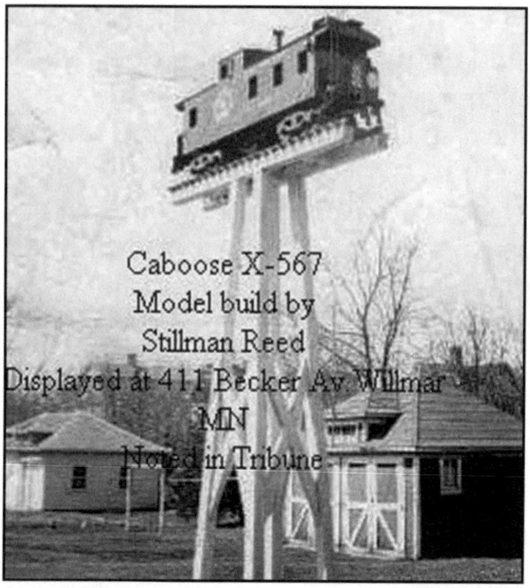

Red Caboose in Willmar, MN (ca 1940)

otherwise provided. Three shorts when the train is standing still means it is going to back up. And four shorts is the call for signals, or instructions. Two long blasts means that the engineer is ready to get going, and one long blast tells the crew they area approaching the station or a crossing.

Railroad men's swearing is prevalent but they used a lot of slang too. Here are some nutty expressions: the caboose about which I wrote a while back called the crummy, hack or parlor car. The Telegrapher is the brass pounder because the telegraph key is always made of brass. A string of brownies are freight cars, a gandy dancer is a man who works as a section man keeping track of the condition of the tracks over a certain area. There were many more but I have forgotten them.

I have neglected to say that Jim Hill's Great Northern Railway is the one that transected our little town. Business of the railway there was transacted by a Mr. William Corkins, the depot agent, so called. He was a tall stately sort of person and every one liked him. His sojourn as agent lasted many years.

The depot with its large waiting room provided with benches that were perverse to adding to the comfort of ones anatomy, was a stop over for kids on the north

Telegraph Desk a standard in Great Northern Depots

Great Northern Depot, Cokato, Minn

William H. Reed Drayman in White Shirt

side ,and a half way mark to home. Here kids and grownups alike would await the arrival of the passenger trains to see who had been somewhere or who was going "aboard". Seeing the old wood and coal burner pull into the station and brake to a stop with an exhaustive wheeze of steam, was delightful. Many times in winter it was hard for the wheels to grasp he rails and they would go round and round. This was especial true of the loaded freights which would huff and puff to get started. Many times I thought of the old adage, "I think, I can, I think I can, and then finally a burst of satisfaction "I thought I could, I thought I could" when I heard the train struggling for contact.

Many times we kids would "walk" the rails between the depot and the crossing which took us down the road, to home. This was a feat of balance for the inexperienced but lots of fun once, on our way to or from school we found a freight train blocking our way and we would have to wait until it cleared the crossing. At times we would take a chance and crawl under the middle part of the of the car or jump over the air couplings between the cars. We girls had to be extra careful we didn't get our long skirts caught in the process of jumping over. Mother and Dad vary much disapproved of our doing this and of course we seldom said anything about it.

Holidays

Thanksgiving and Christmas celebrations were extra special in our young lives. Easter found us attending church, and we probably spent more time admiring the decorations of lilies and other flowers and the array of new bonnets than in listening to the story of the resurrection. I don't recall having any contacts with the Easter Bunny but we did have colored eggs and plenty of their contents to enhance our meals for days afterwards.

Thanksgiving was nearly always spent with Aunt Mary and Uncle Ed they had more room than we did and could spread out a good long table. More of the relatives attended this time of feasting than at Christmas time, mostly because the weather was not so severe. Mother and some of the others helped provide some of the food and helped prepare the dinner. Besides the big fat turkey, the items I well remember that were different, were the plum pudding and the dried corn. Uncle made the pudding and the corn had been prepared during the fall season. It was cut from the cob and dried in the sun on flat pans, with a piece of gauze over the top of it. When thoroughly dried it was stored in cotton sacks and hung from the ceiling of the pantry until wanted for a meal.

Aunty Mary would put it on to cook early in the morning, as it took hours to get it tender, but it had a flavor so different from fresh corn and everyone liked it. Of course there were the pumpkin and mince pies along with the plum pudding which were served with coffee a bit later, giving our dinners time to "settle" as they called it.

The evening was usually spent nibbling the leftovers and a final gesture on the part of Uncle Ed was bringing in a huge pan full of popped and buttered corn. The celebration ended with the women in the kitchen cleaning up the dishes and pots and pans the men intent in a game of cards and the kids playing tiddlywinks or old maid, sprawled out on the living room floor. A happy time for all.

The Christmas festivities were alternated between the two families. This season for our family was not too exciting as we knew we would get new clothes and shoes instead of a lot of toys, tho some of these, of course, included in the gifts as well as oranges from far off California; apples , nuts and candy. The big heater in the living room served as the fireplace and we would hang our stockings up on the wall behind it.

A small but beautiful Christmas tree graced the living room. This was strung with popcorn which we kids had helped to pop and string, and strings of cranberries, tinsel and small colored balls. Candle holders that clipped on the branches of the tree held small candles that were lit come evening time but extreme caution had to be taken lest the flame set the tree on fire. Many calamities happened because people got careless. When the electric lights for trees came on the market these clip ones were discarded but we missed the soft glow of the candles.

NOTE (Cokato got electrical service in 1913. The Reed home was one of the first to have electricity in the town of Cokato, installed by her brother Stillman who had gone to school in Chicago for electricity. (early 1919), after he returned from World War 1)

One year when Uncle Ed and Aunt Mary were having the family group for Christmas, someone decided to play Santa Claus. One of their living room doors opened on to the porch and Santa Claus came in that way, perhaps a little too quickly as he frightened my little cousin who screamed and kicked all the while Santa was passing out his many gifts to us. I was very small at the time but can well remember the commotion his appearance caused.

Word about Our Neighbors

When we were very small a family of six lived in a small grove of trees across the street. The father worked in a brick yard east of town. The girls were about our age, the boy older. Mrs. Gustafson, yes they were Swedes, was an unusually busy person and kept her house and yard spic and span. Many times she would be out in the yard with the broom sweeping the walks and grounds around the house to keep it clean of leaves and debris.

Later when the house burned down, luckily no one was hurt, they moved into a two story house in the eastern part of town. For quite some time after the fire it was hard going for the Gusafsons, so Mrs. G took in washing and did huge ones, then ironed everything she had washed I shall never forget how I marveled at the manner in which she would roll the clothes after sprinkling them for she got them rolled so tightly you couldn't make a dent in them with your finger.

She was always so kind and when we went to their house to play with the three girls she always fixed a snack for us. She lived to a ripe old age. I went to see her many times after her family had left home and Mr. Gusafson had died. I seemed to be a favorite of hers, and she always greeted me with a broad happy smile.

Other neighbors we had were Finnish people. We kids enjoyed being with these folks, too, as they were lonely and were trying hard to learn the English language. I am sure in some respects that we helped them overcome some of their difficulties with it. Later another Swedish family moved in and we got to know the kids real well. They spoke English as well as we did, and the folks too, though they had the accent peculiar to new comers.

The older son Philip (known to us kids as "Moss" was confirmed with me in the Episcopalian Faith and he in late years became a minister in that denomination. "Peanuts" otherwise know as Carl, His brother, married and moved to Minneapolis where he established a paint store. My brother living not too far from the store went in one day to buy some paint and was much surprised to see his old neighbor in the bosses chair.

On the small hill west of our home stood a large house, with a large family living in it, the Halversons, 12 children, nine boys and three girls. The house sat perched on the hill like a castle minus the domes and turrets but it was a nice place and they had a big beautiful yard which we, as well as other kids, took advantage of even though we had a nice yard of our own. My brother Stillman and Hank, one of his age, acted like a couple of bullies with us girls between times but we new much of the time they were just big bluffs. Of course we likely had something to do with egging them on. Mrs. Halverson straightened them out many times, as did mother.

Mr. Halverson was the owner of the local Tannery where they processed animal hides into leather. Two of the older boys worked with him. The youngest of the three girls, Rhode, and I grew to be good friends, Hank was killed in the first World War.

The Matter of Styles

Clothes didn't mean much to us growing kids and of course we were conformists to a degree. We all wore long ankle length dresses, black stockings (no one had heard of hose) in the winter, white ones in summer if the occasion called for covered legs and feet but for the most time we went barefooted, and loved it, dressing up only on Sunday to go to church or if invited to dinner or if the folks were expecting company. Petticoats we had in abundance, at least two and sometimes three; knee length panties, and camisoles which sufficed as bras. Sometime these were made with flowered ribbons at the top which showed through our sheer blouses. And everyone knew when one had new shoes for they invariably "squeaked" and one felt mighty conspicuous. Dad finally decided he could overcome this predicament. He had a cobblers last (an iron thing shaped like the sole of a shoe, and on a stand) and he put these shoes on it and drove short nails through the soles. This held the inner and outer soles together, their rubbing causing the squeaking, and it really did stop it.

Our bane in was winter trying to get the long legged underwear into our stockings so they didn't bulge around the ankles where it showed. I remember many a time that we would start out from home and out of sight of it would reach in and pull the drawers up to our knees, then redo them enroute home in some protected spot along the way, or in the rest room before we left school. Of course when we grew older the folks let us have knee length undies.

Hair styles were indeed varied, and many different ones did we have over the years. At first curls, and when mother got sick of hearing us yell when she combed out the snarls of a morning she would threaten us and that doing no good she "whacked it off" as she put it and we had bobs and bangs. From then on it was pigtails. As we grew older we began to do our own hair, helping each other if necessary. We always went along with the prevailing fad, once it would be hair ribbons, next a big black taffeta bow at the nap of the neck, then curls down the back or braids which of course depended on the length of the hair.

When I think of the teasing or so called back combing of the hair in the middle 1960's I well recall the time we used to tease the hair over our ears into "biscuits" pulling the rest of it to the back of our heads in a knot, using hair pins to anchor them. One implement that aided us to beautify ourselves was a so called "curling iron" a devise looking much like a metal tongs, a curved hollow tube fitting over a solid one.

It was opened and closed by a U shaped handle that squeezed together to open the tongs. The handle was shaped thusly to more conveniently fit into the lamps glass chimney, to be heated. Care had to be taken not to get I too hot or burnt hair was the result, and this did happen at intervals. After many tries we found the exact heat for a nice curl.

Here I want to say something about the lamps we had. A chore handed to us girls much of the time was to keep the many lamps in good working condition which entailed the following; lamps bowls filled with kerosene and carefully wiped off, wicks turned up and the accumulated carbon trimmed off with a scissors, relit and check to see the flame was burning evenly. Then all chimneys had to have their daily bath in sudsy water to make them shine. Many times when the lamp burned, especially if it was turned up a bit too high soot accumulated on the upper part of the chimney. When night came we forgot about our chore and felt pleased over our efforts to create a soft light and well burning wicks.

Our Toys

The main toys for we girls were dolls, doll buggies, dishes made of crockery which looked like majolica ware, tin dishes and home made doll furniture. Our collection of dolls included a lack rag doll which mother made out of dark blue denim from worn out jeans (overalls in those days) which seemed to be a favorite.(there was no race discrimination in hose days) We seemed undecided about the other dolls, which consisted of cornhusk dolls, clothespin dolls and the kind that one wishes for now the black haired china headed dolls, which became antiques and were very costly The only one that survived the battles of childhood was a prized bisque headed doll belong to my sister (Alice) My sister (Alice) died in her teens (18) and the doll was given to me in later years to keep for posterity. Boys toys were usually trucks, wagons, skates, baseball bats and balls and roller skates. These were sturdy toys an usually lasted several years.

One time mother disposed of a number of chickens she kept n a small henhouse, and told us kid if we would clean and spray it good we could use it for a play house for the present at least. We didn't relish the idea at all but grasped opportunity by it disgusting smell and went to it, cleaning, spraying and scrubbing. Dad (Will) took pity on us and did most of the spraying when he saw we were putting forth unvarnished effort and he helped with the spraying, and then whitewashed the whole thing for us. It really made a nice playhouse after we adorned the walls with pieces of wall paper we had begged from the local dealer.

One thing we loved to do was to take our doll buggies, fill them with doll blankets and then dress our old pussycat and put a bonnet on him and wheeled him around in the buggy. He had as much fun as we did.

The Part Music Played in Our Lives

When I was about ten years old my folks bought a lovely square, rosewood piano, much like the small baby grand's. My musical background was well founded from early childhood, so when Dad brought the piano home on the big dray, along with several men to help get it unloaded I was really thrilled.

I started on the musical ladder with mother doing the first teaching. Before that time I would pick out tunes on my grandmother's organ and she would show me what keys to use and how to pump the pedals. I also played on Aunt Mary's organ "playing by ear", in other words playing tunes made up as I played, without the help of sheet music or books.

My first paid music teacher was the old maid daughter of the harness maker of the town. Her name was Esther Haugland, and was the skirt and blouse type of person. She was very nice but many times I did revile against the manner in which she taught me. The scales were endless with no variation in the least, up and down, and over and over. All that for a payment of only 50 cents an hour, but that even was big pay in those days. But she evidently had a case in point. I have her to thank for a lifetime of piano playing and I heartily give her credit for it. Little did I realize that I would be playing for many long years and this training was invaluable when I took a notion in later years to learn how to play the violin. Mother played well too and we often played duets. My brother (Stillman) and sister (Alice) also took lessons when they were old enough, but gave up before they got a good start.

The Weekly Band Concert

In the center of the city park was an open air bandstand, built high above the ground so everyone could see what was going on up there and could watch the conductor wave his wand beating time for the musicians. A bandstand and uniformed players with their shining instruments was intriguing to the towns youngster and enjoyed immensely by the oldsters. It was a wonder to us kids how a big fat fellow could swell up his cheeks and make music by blowing into that funny shaped instrument called a bass horn, or how the fellow with the slide on his horn could make music when there were no buttons to press. Also it was fun to guess when the drummer would bang the big drum with the padded drum stick.

Doctor Ahlstrom, a dentist, was the conductor of the band. He was a small fellow, thin faced, and wore glasses. He was a good dentist too. Perhaps his proficiency in pulling teeth was the reason he could extract such beautiful music out of his volunteer musicians. The fellows would practice one evening during the week in the upper story of the City Hall and when the wind was blowing from the southeast we could hear it there at home. Our home was only a few blocks from the park and evenings when the folks didn't feel like dragging us kids down to the park for the concert we would all sit on the back stoop and listen to the music, even if we couldn't see anything, until the hungry mosquitoes drove us in.

School Days............School Days

My Grade and High School teachers, I remember them well. Miss Trogan (Ida) started us kids out in the first and second grades. She was a tall slender, motherly sort of person and every youngsters she ever taught loved her. Our third grade teacher came from a well-to-do family named Swenson, her name being Stella, and she thought she was someone or other. Before she got through the first year she taught she had married the principal, a Mr. Hargrave. For some reason or other she pick on me perhaps because at times I would do a bit of cutting up a trait handed me by my Grandmother (Caroline) Reed.. One day she cracked me on the head with a ruler. I told mother when I got home who in turn sent a sharp note back to miss Swanson.

This didn't help matters any. I was promoted to the fourth grade in the next spring. My fourth grade and fifth grade teacher was a Miss Nelson (Ruth) a real young lady, just out of Normal School as the Teachers' College was called then. We like this young lady and she was good to us, but other than that I don't recall too much about her. My Sixth year teacher brought forth, Alta McVicker, who was strict, straight laced and whose fort was long division, It seemed that was all we learned, though I am sure there were some side "issues". Figures were my bane. I can still see the long ladders of figures going down the paper.

When we reached the 7th grade we found facing a short, buxom, happy person in Nellie Bly Huntley, a wonderful person. We all loved her and were so happy when we learned she would be teaching us in the ninth grade too.

One incident in the 7th grade, long remember, was; Miss Huntley asked on of the girls, a close friend of mine , a question. She stuttered, gulped and after much hesitation and urging from Miss Huntley, finally said "I swallowed it" this started giggles and then outright laughter but perhaps more at Miss Huntley than for what the student had said. She laughed along with the rest of us until the tears rolled down her cheeks and on down her plump bosom, which made it all the funnier to us kids.

Getting into High School found us in a huge room which housed all four of the upper grades, and we were greeted by a number of extra teachers. Two teachers held fourth as principals during the four years, a Miss Minnie Rassmuson, a nice but stern person and no "monkey business" the first two years of her reign.

What a pleasant change the last two years when Miss Mary Thorstrom took over. She was lovable, kind and helpful at any time we needed her, and we needed no admonition from her as to our behavior. Others were Maud Scharff, Home Economics, or as we knew it cooking and sewing; Elsie Collins, Algebra and Geometry; Mr. Knock; what a name for a Swede, and Mr. Lindstrom, Languages (Swedish & German), and of course for the boys instructors in mechanics and woodwork. I got many zeros for nonparticipation in Swedish, the part where I had to translate English into Swedish especially, because most of the kids in the class from homes where Swedish was spoken all the time and I wasn't about to make an asna (donkey in Swede) out of my self. In German I had equal ground so did well.

I liked sewing. Many things presented to us I learned at home such as the different kinds of stitches, seams, hems, etc. And how to operate a sewing machine, the old treadle kind. It was a trick to maneuver the treadle trying to keep you feet going while your hands were busy trying to get the sewing done. My biggest success in this endeavor the second year was making a blue and white sailor suit, so popular then, which was my pride and joy, cooking was a laugh.

Four girls were given a recipe and had to divide it in fourths and each girl did a fourth recipe. You never did know exactly what you had made as there only enough for a wee bit. Four girls could have worked together and had something to eat when it was finished

We had two me principals to oversee the running of the school. One a Mr. Hargrave in the earlier years of our schooling nearly lost his job when in the 5th grade a young cut-up got smart and Mr. H. was called to straighten him out. Instead of talking him to the office and thoroughly reprimanding him he grabbed the boy by the neck and seat of the of the breeches, yanked him out of his seat- the kid was sure fighting- and threw him bodily up against the slate blackboard. The irate parents all but asked him to resign so after that there was little funny stuff pulled, and the "Head man" stayed out of sight most of the time, as did our second principal,

Mr. Pickard who only showed himself to the student body for speech making or reprimands.

We girls were made to believe that my brother (Stillman) and a couple of bigger fellows gave him the "works" a couple of times.

One extra curricular part of our school work was a girls basketball team. I joined up and was enthusiastic about it until someone banged me on the nose causing a bad nosebleed and then I chickened out deciding it was a bit rough for me.

The old High School was built in the late 1800's of red brick, a square sort of severe looking building with lots of windows. It had a dome on the roof which held a bell and you just didn't ignore the call of that bell. No elevator to raise us to the second floor, but two flights of wide stairs exercised our young limbs, one from the main entry to the first floor and another double one to the second. The first floor housed grades 1 to 6 and the upper floor was divided into one large class room for the 7th an 8th grades; a couple of rooms for class study and for Home Economics.

Then the large high school room for four upper grades. Here we were dished out English, History, Languages, Mathematics, Physics and chemistry. Shorthand, typing and bookkeeping were offered only during the three winter months, and were know as short courses, along with other studies which he boys living in the country who had to help spring and fall with farm chores, could take advantage of. These were available too to the regular students.

Cokato Public School, built in 1902 with an addition in 1910, was destroyed by fire in 1917.

(Brother Stillman worked as a carpenter on the rebuilding of the school)

During most of the four years in High School a girl by the name of Francis Heed, and I, whose name was Reed, were selected to play the incoming and outgoing marches which were a part of the regular program. We would take turns. We also played for the songs we sang and took part in a Glee Club in which many, and good singers participated. Let me mention here that we always had pledge to the flag and prayer before classes started.

When I finally graduated there were only sixteen in our class, twelve girls and four boys, who had survived the rigors of education.

Mother had wanted me to go to Normal School (in St. Cloud) but I was a highly nervous individual, having been broken from left to right handedness and I told her I just couldn't teach because the minute the kids got unruly I would knock their heads together. The she wanted me to be a music teacher same thing there. I had taken shorthand and typing during the short courses so after graduating I wound up taking Business administration in college and did make a good secretary. The same year I graduated the school was gutted by fire but it was quickly rebuilt and in time for school in September.

Were We Ever Sick

Well, we certainly were! We had all of the communicable diseases going except small pox. The Scarlet Fever we had was called scarletine, a milder form of the disease. When I was ten I nearly died because I was too stubborn to say anything about having a sore throat. One morning when I was ready for school I was talking with mother, no doubt noting that I had a queer sound in my voice mother asked "Is your throat sore?" I denied it but being a wary mother she decided to have a look anyway. "Heaven" she said, "it looks like diphtheria" for I had white spots on the sides of my throat indicative of the dreaded malady.

I was put to bed and Dr. Peterson called. On looking at my throat he said "Ya, she's got diphtheria all right" So I was given a shot of antitoxin via an ugly looking needle, as were my brother (Stillman) and sister (Alice), also being kept home from school. I was a sick girl but it evidently wasn't my time to let go of my earthly connections. My brother (Stillman) and Sister (Alice), weren't sick but fretted for having to be tied at home. One thing we didn't like was the big old sign put on the front of the house with "Quarantine" on it, to keep everyone aware of contagion within.

Two weeks before I gradated from High School I again had a bout with the grim reaper. I had acute appendicitis but thanks to the two wonderful doctors; Kvello and Flom Freed, that had established their business in Cokato, I'm Still alive. My grandmother (Caroline) was in on the consultation as to whether to operate or not and said "Oh she will die."

I told her even if didn't go to the hospital I would die anyway. I was taken to the hospital in the middle of the night my cousin. The hospital was an old home owned by a family of well to do folks, converted into a place for the sick, so the operating room was on the second floor. I wasn't able to walk up the long stairs so my cousin "threw" me over his shoulder and deposited me on a table in the operating room. By the time I had passed into oblivion and woke up all bandaged up in my room. As I convalesced my sister (Alice) and a close friend would come up and the two cutups would get me to laughing which was a mighty painful ordeal. About the time I was ready to go home, Dr. Kvello's brother was operated on and I shall always remember how he swore when coming out of the ether, and I still wonder now an the what I said or did.

Hospital Cokato, Minn

REED
Alice Myrtle Marie and Elsie Lillian Florence

I missed the baccalaureate service but did get to the graduation ceremonies at the Lutheran Church. Of course the whole town knew that I had been ill and afterwards many said "how in the world did you march all the way down the aisle" I had to explain that I hadn't. The class had been designated to sit in the choir paws which were placed in the front of the big pipe organ close to the chancel. I was taken to the rear of the organ and directed as to where to sit and when most f the graduates got o their paces, still standing, I slipped into my seat. During the reception I was given a chair to sit on.

All went well until fall when another sickness hit. My sister (Alice) had contacted typhoid fever, so called walking typhoid as she had been tired much of the time but didn't realize what was causing it. Later she went from Morris where we lived to Cokato to visit Aunt Mary and Uncle Ed and there she succumbed to the disease. My graduation dress was used to bury her in.

Mother was a good nurse during our confinements over the early years and we had help from Grandmother (Caroline) too. She was great on using all kind of herbs, recipes handed down several generations. Every spring we got sulphur and molasses, sarsaparilla and a number of other potions I've forgotten the name of. When real small we had to wear at intervals a little sack of asaphidity which stunk to high heaven. Mother would put a small piece in a thin cloth, tie a string to it and loop it around our necks. What it warded off I don't know but it was supposed to be a preventative.

One affliction I had, though not an illness, though it really should come under that category, was homesickness. When I see a youngster who is home sick I feel badly for him. For many ears I bawled the minute my mother got out of sight, especially at night. At that time she belonged to the Eastern Star and Royal Neighbors and when she went to a lodge meeting I would lay awake until she returned though she never knew it.

Cokato Order of Eastern Star Lodge 179
Emily Reed Matron center Aunt Mary Taylor far right

During the summer months of my high school days. I decided I wanted to make some money so want to a farm house a number of miles away, but every night I cried my eyes out. After few tries I decided, with Mother's consent, that my feelings were dearer to me than the small stipend received for my labors. I think it was $5.00 a week and my room and board. I finally broke the habit or stigma when I stayed with some close friends of the family while away at college.

Our Pet Cats

Our pets were few. Outside of having the two horses of Dads to love, we had cats. Grandmother (Caroline) wouldn't tolerate a dog around. She would raise her voice to a high pitch if she saw one near the fence or in the yard but did condescend to let us have cats. Two cats in particular stand out in my memory.

At one time we had a small cute kitten which my brother (Stillman) took a special liking to and claimed as his own, but tragedy stalked. My mother had one rail barrel in the shed for handy use and a cover was made for the top of it, which cover was supposed to be closed over the barrel at all times as a small place in the wall above the barrel had been left open for the cat to come and go at will the barrel ld being his landing place. One morning my brother (Stillman) went out the back door, and almost immediately came back into the kitchen his arm doubled up over his face. We thought he had banged into the door as he went out but with his arm still over his face (he was crying) he pointed in the direction of the rain barrel in the shed. Mother rose to the occasion and went to see what the trouble was. There on top of the water floated my brother's little cat, drowned because someone had forgotten to put the lid on the barrel after getting water, and the cat jumping into the space left for him didn't find his usual solid landing place. we all had a good cry but mother was put out because she was minus a nearly full barrel of soft water, a precious thing right then as rainstorms had been few and far between.

One tabby or tiger cat we kids owned was a personage for certain. He was family cat and we all loved him, even Dad, for the cat kept the mice cleaned out of the grain barrels in the barn, Tom as we called him, was definitely a house cat. We could do anything with him and he never scratched us even when we put doll clothes on him. H favorite "resting" place was on top of the piano. In those days everyone kept a half dozen family pictures on top o the piano. Old Tom would jump upon the keyboard and then to the top of the piano careful to see that he didn't knock any of the pictures over. Then he would curl up and with one eye shut would keep the other one open to see what was gong on and if interested him would then meander through the pictures again and on down to the place of activity.

If he wished out at night he would let us know for he would walk the length of the keyboard quickly playing a little tune a he went, We all knew the signal and someone would get up and let him out. When he wanted back in he would scratch on the screen or if in winter and storm windows had replaced the screens e would wait up a few minutes and then go to the door and he was ready to come in. He succumbed to the rigors of old age many years later and we really did miss the old fellow.

Businessess and Business Men in Cokato That I Remember

Cokato had a number of places of business and they all seemed to be well patronized; Two drug stores, two grocery stores, two hotels, a jewelry store, two banks, two or three general stores that carried dry goods so called anything from woman's dresses, to men's and boys suits, shoes, hats, etc. One of these also had a grocery store connected with it. There were a couple of butcher shops, a flour mill, two hardware stores, three grain elevators and a canning factory which at first just canned corn during the month of August. Later years the processed peas and pumpkin, and then had a rival canning company a few blocks to the west. Though really not businesses in the sense of the word Cokato was graced with four churches; Lutheran, Baptist, Episcopalian and Mission. These tended to spiritual necessities of the community. For a small town of around 1000 inhabitants this was a good representation of people and businesses serving the public.

Henry C. Bull was the head of the one bank then in operation, tho another went into business across the street. Mr. Bull was a congenial person. He would stop anywhere and talk to grownups and kids alike. Being in the "upper crust" category Mrs. Bull entertained in their lovely home, with aid of a maid, but she often asked us kids to come over when we were visiting Uncle Ed and Aunt Mary who lived next door to them. In spite of their money she was a very friendly lady and seemed to enjoy our talks with her.

Mr. Bull had a fine carriage and two beautiful horses. At the rear of the Bull home was a big barn in which the horses were stabled and Mr. Bull hired a caretaker that was a gem in our minds. We never did learn his last name so we just called him "Charley Bull".

Many times when we drummed up an excuse to swing around to Uncle Eds to see if he had concocted any special tidbits of food, we would go down the alley, past the Bull barn hoping the horses would be inside. Sometimes Carrley would be at Uncles when we got there. He and Uncle Ed did a lot of visiting and many times we would inveigle Charley to take us into the barn so we could pet the horses.

Many years later the Bulls retired and moved to California. The property was sold several times and finally became a mortuary, part of the old home being used for living quarters by the mortician. The beautiful gardens were neglected and finally all was put into lawn. The old barn ad long since been torn down.

Western House, one of the two hotels in town was an up-to-date hotel, several stories high, built of red brick in the style of the Brownstone front buildings in the east. Charley Carlson, better known to everyone by C. M. a bachelor, and his old maid sister Carrie, ran the hotel.

They were well liked folks and even we kids would stop in the hotel lobby now and then for a chat with one of the other of them. usually the sister as Charley was out around drumming up customers especially at train time.

The competing hotel there was run by a widower and his maiden niece, the Runions. Lizzie, as Miss Runions was called, was also a music teacher and the organist of the Episcopal church Miss Runions was chubby to the point of being buxom while in contrast Miss Carlson was the tall slender, typical old maid type.

The hotels were only half a block or so from the depot, one south the other east and they served .well t many weary salesmen. After many long years of service the Western House closed its doors and for quite some time stayed vacant. At this writing the Cokato Hotel is still in business with more modern accommodations now and then making it a most desirable place to stay in.

The Western House was finally purchased by a local business man and turned into the Cokato Produce Company where eggs, chickens and turkeys were processed. Farmers from all over the county brought their poultry and eggs to the Produce Company.

The Henry C. Bull Home
(This is the funeral home Emily's wake was held.)

Which they in turn sold to stores in Cokato and merchants in the small towns around. It was an establishment not condoned by the towns people, because in the summer especially, the undesirable aroma from the place made for lots of vitriolic conversation, and had the conversations been effective the whole setup would have been moved out of town before it got going good. However, the owner was a "big shot" around town, so the town council did nothing about it. This thorn in the side of the populous was enhanced by the stench coming from the place close to the Produce Company where pelts were processed and made into leather. It was called the Tanning Factory or Tannery but little machinery was used, most of the work being done by men with hand instruments used for the purpose.

Finally after many years, to the relief of the residents, the Produce Company wanted to expand and so bought property out at the edge of town and moved the stinking mess out there. Not long afterward the Tannery closed down too for lack of work as many people preferred the work done in the big city Minneapolis.

A Canning Factory (now know as Minnesota Valley, home of the Green Giant) was begun by some of the business men of the town. They bought land adjoining our property and were at first disturbed about having them there but when it was finally built the grounds were landscaped and it looked like a big apartment house, made of red brick, too, and there was no activity except in the business office, until fall when the corn was ready for canning.

The building of this structure was a fascinating bit of concern to us kids. Every day we were in about the slow rising factory, our curiosity nosing its way to find out what was going on I can well appreciate what some of those workmen would have liked to have done with us.

When the yawning retorts were being installed one man threatened to shut us in one of them but our faith in humans was not the least bit shaken, in fact we sort of felt it might be fun to get into them. However they were deep and though we could have slid down into them easily, getting out would have been a problem without the use of a ladder or its equivalent. Large cages of cans filled with cans of corn were lowered by crane into the retorts and the covers pulled down. They then look like huge presser cookers.

Long open sheds were built adjacent to the main building which housed the machinery. Into the open sides of this building (doors could be let down at night) many tons of corn from the huge wagons were dumped in so the huskers could get to it easily. In the shed each person who wished to husk corn, even the young kids who were big enough to hold the ears of corn, were given a bushel basket and a card. When the basket was full of husked corn the foreman would punch a hole in the card, each punch representing the magnificent price of 10 cents and it seemed like it took forever to get all the numbers punched out of the card at which time we took it to the cashier and received our remuneration.

No one seemed to mind being paid a pittance for their work for it was fun and gave the participants a chance to visit with each other and pass the gossip around. A receiving bin for the husked corn was built in the center of the shed where a number of girls sat and who checked the corn for any defects, silks, and maybe cut out a spot where a worm had decided to get a meal, then they would throw the corn into a chute with a conveyer in it which took the corn to the cutters in the main building.

There the corn went through the process of cooking and canning. At the end of the filler line a soldering machine sealed the cans and they were then dropped into the cages for the retorts. Coming out of the retorts the cages were moved by crane to the are house to be packaged, (boxed and labeled) 24 cans to a case and then loaded as orders came in into railroad cars se out on their short spur track for shipment. When the days canning was done all parts of the machinery, conveyer belts and receiving bins were cleaned by live steam and many times we could hear the sizzling way into the nite.

When automatic huskers were installed in a newly designed building many folks regretted this fact and talked about the many hundreds of ears of corn they had husked over the years, in reminiscing about the good old days.

Other Businesses: Mabusth (see Narrative and picture in the final chapter) and Thelandr were names that somehow didn't seem to fit in with the Swede Olson's, Johnson's, Petersons, etc.. However these two merchants dealt in dry good so called.. men's and women's ware, yard goods, boots and shoes. Mr. Mabusth had a cobbler at the rear of his store for needed shoe repair. Mr. Thelander also had a grocery the rear of his store. There were the accustomed barrels of crackers, pickles and pickled herring called "sill" A huge wheel of cheese graced one end of the counter from which the grocer cut wedges as ordered, usually giving the purchaser a thin slice to get the flavor.

Prices would astound people these days. Here are a few examples. Sugar 20 pounds for $1.00, Rice 25 Pounds for $1.00 English walnuts, 8 pounds for $1.00, One gallon can of apples 10 cents, Strawberry Jelly 5 cents a pound. Butter was cheap and was usually sold in 2 to 5 pound crocks, the crock included.

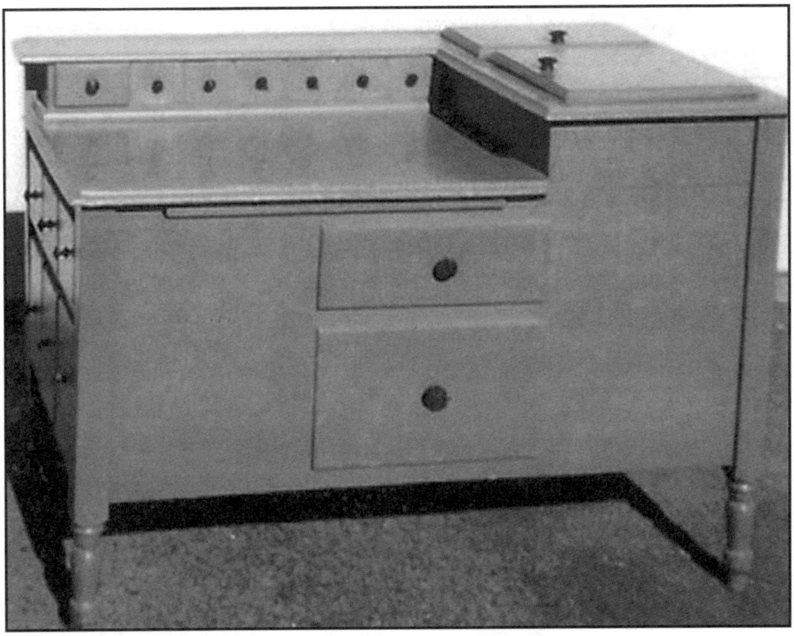

Cabinet was used by family from the late 1890's

(Mother Emily would place a 5 pound crock of butter on the bread board, and added salt to it, which added taste and kept the butter from becoming rancid, then she returned the butter to the crock for use).

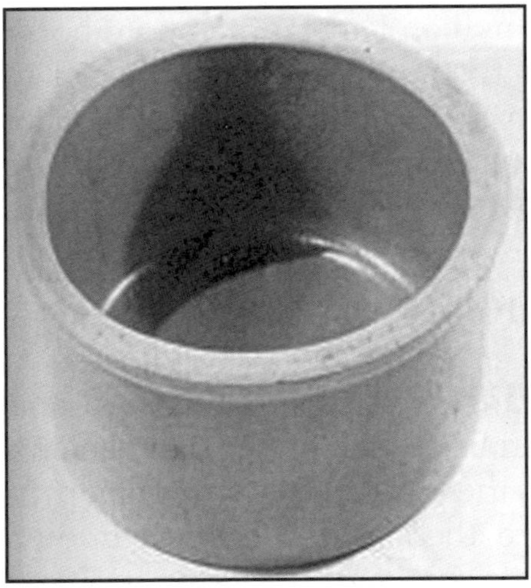

2 pound Butter Crock

Meat was cheap too. We kids loved to shop with mother and were sometimes sent to do the shopping by ourselves when we grew older.

The two drug stores were kept busy. A Mr. Peterson, whose initials were A. P. but always known by them, had a store on one corner of the main street and Theodore Swanberg on the other. Theodore was quite a bit younger and would always spend time gabbing with us kids when we had an occasion to get something at the drug counter or other supplies he carried.

The officiating general medical practitioner was Dr. Peterson, no relation to A. P but who had a small dingy looking office above the Drug store. However, Doc was a good one and we liked him. The doctor who tended to our eyes lived in Dassel, a town six miles to the west making trips to Cokato a couple of times a week or when someone called him for his services.

One of the interesting spots we kids love to visit was the blacksmith shop. Here a big swarthy fellow, always wearing a heavy canvas apron, worked with shaping horse shoes, repairing farm tools and sometimes small pieces of farm machinery along with items like skates and hoes. We would sand in awe as he worked the bellows to make the coals hotter and then take the red hot irons from the fire, lay them on the anvil and shape them into horse shoes, then he would toss them into a bucket of water to "steel" them. He was also the "wainright", a repairer of wagons, and the wheels of those wagons. Every village had a blacksmith for he was an indispensable citizen in those days.

The men's selected place, the Barber Shop, was well patronized. The site of this shop was indicated to home folks as well as strangers in town by the red and white striped pole with a round knob on top, conveniently placed at the side of the door. (The barbershop in Cokato had a case where the patrons kept their own personal cup that held their soap and brush for applying lather for a shave.)

William H. Reeds' cup showing Trade(Drayman,Teamster now.).

The barbershops were popular places not only for getting a shave, haircut and perhaps for shaping up of a goatee, beard or muttonchops, as sideburns were then called, but it was a place for relaxation and sociability in which men liked to linger. Here they could mingle with the boys without the fear of feminine intrusion, hear the latest news and maybe take part in some fine singing which no doubt had something to do with the beginning of the popular Barbershop Quartets over the country.

The Post Office as next door to the Barber shop and just a block from the depot. You had a mail box there with a combination lock on it or called for your mail at the General Delivery window. Letter postage was 2 cents and postcards 1 cent. A daily trip was made to the Post Office whether mail was expected or not. Incoming mail was dropped off by the flier. It was interesting to watch the delivery of the sack of mail as the train did not stop or even slow down. A post with an arm on it extended to the edge of the track. As the train came by the arm automatically caught the mail bag which the baggage man on the train held out as the train passed the post. It was a split second maneuver. There seldom was a miss and if there was the mail was scattered for blocks.

Of course I must mention the "Enterprise" the weekly newspaper which carried the comings and goings of the town inhabitants and those around the county.

It also carried an "insides", a sheet of printed news and general information on world affairs that came from the printers in Minneapolis. This sheet was inserted in the paper after the local printing was done. The City Hall, located right across the street from the Enterprise furnished council and other news along with legal advertising, obituaries, announcements, etc. The paper arrived in the mail boxes on Thursday morning and we all looked forward to reading about the happenings in the community.

Gust Akerlund was the town's photographer. His studio was very small, well lighted, and was located on a side street. He was a short, stocky Swede with a broken accent which made him all the funnier to us kids. He did take good pictures with his camera, a large box contraption that stood on legs, with a cord and bulb hanging down by the side of it. He would cover his head with a black cloth, stand at the back of the camera until he had the pose he felt was correct and becoming, then would transfer some slide and squeeze the bulb. He had the art of "posing" people to look like they had starch in their necks and straight jackets under their clothing, and the expressions on the faces of those doing the posing would indicate to the viewer that they saw a funeral procession passing before them. However, he was a popular "picture taker" and did well in the small town.

In the center of one of the down town blocks was a small shop known as the Millinery Shop which was owned and operated by two spinster ladies. They would get the hat "shells" made of buckram (a sort of stiff porous material) and shaped to several different head sizes from the millinery manufacturers in Minneapolis, along with flowers (artificial, usually made of silk and velvet) tulle (a delicate silk lace or netting), veiling, velvet and satin, taffetas and cross grain ribbons.

They were always busy as the woman would flock there to buy beautiful creations sold so cheaply, sometimes as low as $1.50. Anything from big floppy hats with wide brims to the small head hugging types. When spring and Easter came you could tell who had lately been patronizing this shop.

The Local harness maker, father of my music teacher, had a store with a work shop in the back. He sold new harness and he had made, along with belts, straps and other leather goods. He also repaired any leather articles that needed it. You could enter the store blindfolded and knew where you were for the aroma of leather was so apparent it almost hurt your nose. Sometimes he would condescend to give us small scraps of leather from his waste bucket. Most of the time these ended up as stone holders for our sling shots.

A block from our home was an old feed mill. Years before I was born an old German by the name of Seidl built and ran this mill. After he died his two old maid daughters took over the management. Lena, the older, was a tall, thin typical old maid, while Emma was short and chubby. Lena took care of the business end of things at the mill while Emma relived her and took care of the mother and the home which was a small residence not far from the mill. Lena and Emma were quite some dames and I will say, with a fit of nostalgia that we kids liked them. When business wasn't rushing they would knit or ply their needles in fancy work. We girls would go over after school at least a couple of times a week to see how their embroidering was coming along and as they could they taught us many stitches and we made a number of articles under their direction.

They were indeed German and it was too bad that I didn't learn a bit more of it from them, but when minds are young other things seem to be more important.

We spent many happy hours in that old mill, sliding down the grain sacks or plowing through the bins of grain in our bare feet, squealing when we unearthed a mouse buried in the grain enjoying his daily meal.

In the winter we would stop in to warm up a bit though in reality it was just a short block to home. In the summer it was a stop to cool off and fill our noses with the fresh aroma of newly ground grain and perhaps a " kuchen" just out of the oven which to our delight was shared with us. This perhaps was the real reason for stopping.

Years later I felt a tinge of sadness when mother wrote that Lena had died and later that Emma had succumbed and then that the old mill had been torn down to make a way for a modern filling station. It just wasn't the same street without that old mill.

And last but not least I must mention the old jeweler who occupied a small, narrow shop on main street. His name was Johnson and we were told by Dad that his first name was Fiddler tho I am sure he had another but this name came from him being an excellent fiddler of old time tunes. He died before we were old enough to know him. However we did know the one who late bought his business, a fellow by the name of Henry Engstrom. Many times when we would pass his store he would be sitting on a bench on the outside. Sometimes we would be invited into view the many beautiful pins, watches, rings, silverware and would watch him as he inspected the inside of a watch to determine the reason it didn't run.

Neglected Items

And now I have about concluded the history of my early childhood. I am sure I have forgotten things which should have been mentioned but after so many years has passed this is little wonder.

One or two items I neglected that I feel are important are listed on the following couple of pages....

Number one: we had no bathroom when I was real young and taking a bath in those days would make people now laugh their heads off. At lease the hardware companies still sell the sort of tub we had to contend with. A good sized galvanized tin tub, about a foot and a half deep and perhaps three feet across was brought out on Saturday nights for the weekly scrub down, tho we got a daily going over too. Usually the water was used for all three kids, first we girls then my brother as he usually was the dirtiest. Okay!

First we sat down in the tub with legs overboard as we couldn't cram our whole anatomy into that small space, then when we had been scrubbed we were rinsed off by mother with a pan of warm clean water, then proceeded to get our legs taken care of. Of course when we were real small we fitted nicely into the tub.

Number two: I didn't include the spot where mother did most of her relaxing. This was a good sized hammock of woven material, that hung between the house and a big elm tree just the right distance away from the house to conveniently accommodate the hammock.

The elm furnished abundant shade. Midmorning mother would hang the hammock up and anyone that came along could enjoy it. That is if someone wasn't already occupying it, usually someone besides mother. We kids would dump each other out of it if we could catch the occupant unawares. But mother had precedence. She would always have an armful of mending or stocking to darn but enjoyed the cool shade even with busy hands. Evening when we listened to the band concerts of a Saturday night we kids would sit in the hammock, cutting up, poking each other, to be sometimes reprimanded by the folks to quiet down. At night the hammock was taken down, and stored in the shed.

Number Three: The coffee grinder was another important adjunct to the kitchen paraphernalia. Mother always brought a certain blend of coffee beans rather than having the grocer grind it for her. The coffee beans were placed in a cup shaped container at the top of the grinder and mother or one of us kids would grind just enough for a meal or two. Mother always beat up an egg to mix with the grounds as she felt it made better coffee and it did though it took a little longer to "settle" it. I still have the old grinder. In later years mother bought a new-fangled grinder and the old one was put on the shelf until I asked if I could have it. It still is a reminder of the "good old days"

I am putting this in writing so that my grand-children and mayhap my great grand children will read and wonder what made us happy in those years long ago.

Unique Photographs Plus Narratives

In this chapter additional information and photographs are included with some references to the text and also pictures of the family members.

GENTRY
Greek E. and Elsie Florence

GENTRY
25th Anniversary
9 November 1946

GENTRY
Elsie Lillian Florence (Reed) and Ephraim Greek
Married 9 November 1921
Two children

GENTRY
Eugene Greer and Paul Reed

REED
Stillman (Andre) Andrew Prescott and Alvena Fedela (Omlie)
Married 19 August 1922
Two children

REED
Betty Lou and William Vernon

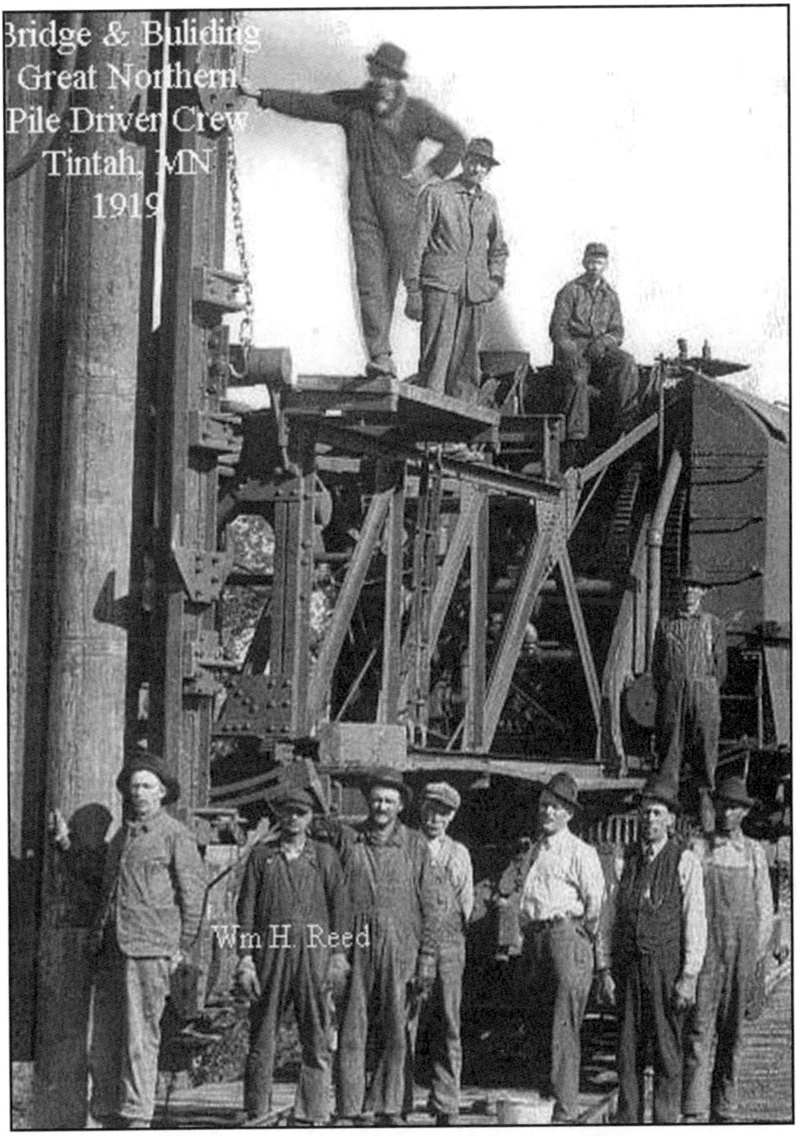

B & B Crane Crew at Tintah Minnesota (ca1919)
William H.A. Reed worked for the Bridge and Building Department. He moved his family to Morris Minnesota while working at Tintah and other jobs west of Willmar

COFIELD
Anna Rebecca (Bukebak) and Orrin Lorenzo

Will Reed Dray

DRAYING

Transferring and Hauling of all kinds to all parts of the city. Rates reasonable. Many years experience. Leave orders at G. N. Depot or telephone 67 or 81.

Will Reed

Prop. Dray Line COKATO

In the Cokato Enterprise July 1910

CITY DRAY

Dray and transfer and general team work. Our rates are reasonable and our service efficient. Phone 136, or G. N. depot.

E. W. PICKRUHN
Proprietor

In the Cokato Enterprise 1919

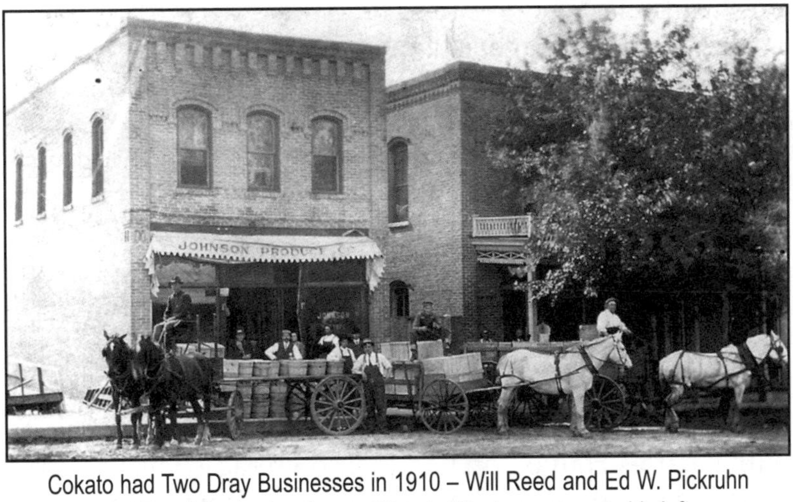

Cokato had Two Dray Businesses in 1910 – Will Reed and Ed W. Pickruhn
Will Reed Center leaning on Wheel. His dray wagon to his left.

Radios Come to Cokato

The reception was fuzzy, the antenna took a while to set up, and the equipment at the telephone office caused too much interference. Despite these hurdles, in the summer of 1922, a new technological wonder was introduced to the people of the town. In 1922, radios came to Cokato.

On Memorial Day, 1922, representatives from the Westinghouse Electric Company, out of Minneapolis, set up a "radio outfit" to show area residents the wonders of this new marvel. Reception was not ideal however, due to interference from the equipment at the telephone office. A later attempt fared better, and listeners could hear the faint signal of WAA in St. Paul.

Less than two months after the people from Westinghouse made their demonstration, the A. L. Thelander store purchased their own radio. Set up by representatives from the American Radio Company, the Cokato /Enterprise/ noted that this radio would receive "anything broadcasted [sic] from any point in the United States." The Enterprise noted the excitement of the community over this new invention, stating that: "There is nothing 'rarin' to go as is radio at the present time; it is the most modern, wonderful tool of modern progress."

Thelander's radio showed its value on election night, 1922, as residents came and went until 2:00 a.m. to hear results. Local electrician, Arnold Johnson, who along with Charles Halvorson had their own radio, also set up a listening station in Walter Harkman's repair shop.

Gradually, the number of stations receivable in Cokato grew, including ones in Chicago (WLS), Denver (KOA), and Yankton (WNAX). The most popular one that could be heard on the local radios was based in Minneapolis, and went by the call signal WLAG. Later this station would be purchased by the Washburn Crosby Company, a prominent Minneapolis flour mill. They renamed the station after themselves, a name that still applies today: WCCO.

By the late 1920s, the popularity of radios exploded across the country, and soon every household had at least one. Quaint as this may sound to a modern audience, the entire family would gather around the radio to hear a concert by a symphony orchestra, listen to election results, or to enjoy the many weekly "serials." Anticipation would grow as the announcer said: "Who knows what evil lurks in the heart of men. The Shadow knows." Or another favorite, set to the William Tell Overture: "Return with us to those thrilling days of yesteryear." So began the weekly adventures of Clayton Moore as The Lone Ranger, with his sidekick, Tonto.

The power of this new medium was best exemplified by an incident on October 1938. H. G. Wells classic book, /War of the Worlds/, told of an invasion of Earth by Martians. A production of this book by the Mercury Theatre Company, headed by Orson Welles, was done so effectively that untold listeners across the nation actually believed the Earth had been invaded.

In addition, who could forget President Franklin Roosevelt and his "fireside chats." Edward R. Murrow gave Americans a first-hand view of the bombing of London by Germany during World War II. And Milton Berle solidified his personna as "Uncle Miltie" with his comedy/variety shows.

Locally, radios were initially sold by the general store merchants like Thelander and Mabusth. Eventually, stores geared specifically towards electronics came into existence. Later these stores would carry other items, like radios supposed replacement—television.

While no radio stations ever arose in Cokato, ones in Litchfield, Hutchinson, and Buffalo worked to serve area communities like Cokato. But for many, there was only one station worth listening to—the afore mentioned WCCO.

It was said that a person flying over Minnesota could tell when the WCCO 10:00 p.m. news ended, because after that, all the house lights went dark as people went to bed. So who kept all those people awake at that hour? Cedric Adams.

In his book, /When 'CCO Was Cookin'/, former WCCO on-air personality Dick Champan noted how the popularity of Adams stretched across the entire Upper Midwest. How appropriate that he was a special guest and emcee for the talent show at the first Cokato Corn Carnival in August 1950.

Despite the growth of other forms of entertainment: television, cinema, home rentals, video games, et. al., radios remain an integral part of our society. Every car has one. Every office has at least one. Every home has at least one also, it not more. Music, political chatter, news and information, and lots of sports can be found across the AM and FM dials. As the 21st century progresses, it is hard to believe that radio will disappear any time soon.

This article first appeared in the October 2004 (V. 24 No. 4) edition of /In The Midst Of/.

Great Northern Railroad Depot

A scattering of claim shanties on some high ground just west of a small creek. This is how a visitor to Cokato would have described the young (and yet un-named) settlement in the summer of 1867. Transportation to points near and far was by horse or ox-cart. A trip to Minneapolis could have taken as long as four days. But only two short years later, this assemblage stood on the verge of becoming a thriving village. Why? Because the railroad had come to town.

In the summer of 1868, the First Division of the St. Paul & Pacific Railroad, which later became Great Northern and eventually Burlington Northern, built a line from Lake Junction (just west of Minneapolis) to Howard Lake. The next year, the line was stretched an additional forty-nine miles from Howard Lake to Willmar. At the fifty mile mark, a station was constructed and a railway official (whose name has never been known) named it "Cokato," after the Dakota word "co-ka-ta."

This first depot was a simple structure built on the north side of the tracks near where Millard Avenue would later cross. J. E. (Ed) Jenks was appointed first station master.

The role railroads played in the development of Cokato is undeniable. Had the railroad followed its original path, near Collinwood Lake, Cokato would have never come into existence. With trains being the only mode of transport in those days, to be passed by was not good news for a settlement.

Typical of any frontier railroad town, Cokato built itself around the tracks and depot. Hotels were never more than a short walk from the station, and the streets all radiated outward from the tracks. Grain elevators sprung up like a line of Easter Island statues along the side tracks. The post office was only a block away to accommodate the man who had to twice daily pull the cart-load of mail from the station to the office.

That original depot, built in 1875, was a simple structure, described by the Cokato Observer as "barn-like." By 1890, the depot had begun to show its age, but despite the clamor by local citizens and officials, no new depot was in sight. Instead, Great Northern officials decided to refurbish it by adding new siding and an interior paint job.

The Cokato Observer noted its objection to this plan, stating "...Jim Hill [Great Northern president James J. Hill] can't afford to build anything more substantial and our citizens will have to use the...structure for a depot until the next decade." Actually, the depot had to suffice for over two decades. Finally, in July 1912, the railroad agreed to build a new depot in Cokato the following year.

The new depot was to be built according to the template used by Great Northern for all new depots in small communities. This fact was a source of amusement to the editors of the Dassel Anchor, who commented "the dream of a much better structure because they were 'so nice' to the railroad company will not be realized by our sister village."

As had been the case with the old station, the new structure was a social focal point for the community. Each weekday, as the time approached for the evening westbound train to arrive—if the schedule held, at exactly 7:22 p.m.—a crowd would gather at the depot. Anticipation ran high as people waited for relatives to arrive after a long journey, traveling salesmen would come looking for lodging, and young children would watch to see who had been in the "big city" for the day.

As Carlton Lee wrote in his poem, We'll Meet Again For The Evening Train, "Summer or winter, in sun or rain; My friends and I met the evening train."

Even as cars became the mode of travel, trains still carried thousands of passengers through Cokato. But many saw the future coming, and warned of the day when trains would no longer be the "way to go."

Passenger service came to an end on May 21, 1960, when the Great Northern eastbound No. 10 stopped at the depot at 4:17 a.m. No one got on or off, and the train resumed its journey. The end of an era had arrived, and no one was there to notice, except the station agent..

Freight was still shipped through the depot, but just like with passengers, the amount of freight continued to decrease, and it became too expensive for the railroad to maintain a depot in Cokato—as had happened in so many other small communities.

The Cokato depot officially closed on July 5, 1974, sixty years after it had been built, and 105 years after that rail line was stretched from Howard Lake to Willmar. Waldo Tesch, the last station agent, had the unenviable duty of locking the depot's doors for the final time.

As the depot sat empty, numerous ideas passed by as to its fate. Finally, Howard Page purchased the depot in 1985 and moved it to Dassel where in now houses the Dassel Depot Railroad Museum.

The trains still run though Cokato both day and night, and the engineers will still wave to children like they did in days past. But no longer do people gather in anticipation at the depot for the arrival of "the evening train."

©Cokato Historical Society, 1998 (Inserted with permission of Director)

The Cokato Hospital

(Editors note: This article is in no way intended to be a complete history of the Cokato Hospital. It is only intended to provide a general overview of this venerable institution's story.)

For almost fifty years, a hospital served the people of Cokato and the surrounding townships and communities. Located at the corner of Third Street and Swanson Avenue, just east of downtown, the Cokato Hospital played a vital role by providing much needed medical services. An imposing two-story structure, the hospital was originally built sometime during the late 1880s as a private residence for the A. W. L. Almquist family. The Peter Stevenson family later resided there. The demolition of this structure, beginning in December 2003, gave countless people the opportunity to recall their memories of this place.

The story of the hospital begins in the summer of 1914, when the July 14 edition of Cokato Enterprise announced that local doctor O. A. Kvello purchased the Stevenson home with the intention of turning the structure into a "modern hospital." Kvello also bought one acre of adjoining property. Kvello was not new to Cokato. He had an existing practice, in operation since the fall of 1913.

Work on the hospital began in the late summer of 1914. Kvello and his partner, Dr. Reagan of Minneapolis, stated that they would spare "no expense or effort...in transforming the building into a strictly modern hospital, and that the grounds will be greatly beautified..."

The hospital officially opened on December 7, 1914. A large crowd visited the facility throughout the day, the Enterprise reported. The Stockholm Orchestra provided musical entertainment.

Kvello ran the hospital until September 1917, when it was purchased by the Cokato Hospital Association. The genesis of the association is not clear. Their treasurer's books indicate that in the fall of 1917, they began selling stock shares to finance the purchase. Numerous individuals and institutions bought shares, including Dr. Kvello. The association ran the hospital for just over two years.

In late October 1919, local doctor Oscar (O. J. R.) Freed and a partner purchased the hospital from the association. By all accounts, Dr. Freed was a respected practitioner of medicine, building the hospital into a first-rate facility during his tenure there. Sadly, Freed died in November 1932 at the age of 47. In 1995, Jo Ann Hannah, Dr. Freed's grand-daughter, donated to the museum the bear-skin lap robe he used when making house calls in his carriage.

Following Freed was Dr. Arthur Thompson. Dr. Thompson began operating the hospital in 1934. He purchased the facility outright in December 1936 from Dr. Freed's widow, Agnes. Thompson himself ran the hospital for seventeen years, until early 1951. At that time, for financial reasons, Thompson proposed turning the facility into a rest home.

The Cokato Association for Public Affairs (a forerunner of the Cokato Area Chamber of Commerce) intervened, organizing a drive to build a fund for keeping the hospital open. The unique aspect of the drive was that the association asked not for donations, but for loans—which were to be paid back with interest. In less than two months, the drive netted $43,000. The beneficiary of this effort was Dr. Theodore Greenfield of Delano, who purchased the hospital in late May 1951. Greenfield's time in Cokato lasted just over fifteen years.

The last chapter of the story of the hospital opened in the December 8, 1966 Cokato Enterprise. On page one of that edition, the following statement appeared: "If the Village will operate the hospital, Dr. Greenfield will stay and practice in Cokato. If the Village does not see fit to operate the hospital, Dr. Greenfield plans to terminate his practice in Cokato." The village decided not to act upon Greenfield's offer.

The hospital saw the final babies born there on January 28, 1967, and the last patients the week of February 15, before closing its doors for the final time.

While the actual building survived, and saw a number of uses over the next three decades, for many, the structure would always be know as "the old hospital."

The final post-script for this story arrived in 2003, when--after too many years of decay--the structure was deemed uninhabitable and slated for demolition. The local building inspector estimated that over $300,000 of repairs were necessary to bring the building up to code. It took less than a week for another icon of Cokato's past to fall victim to the wrecking ball.

Cokato's Hotels

In the early morning hours of July 8, 1977, a fire started in one of the rooms of the Cokato Hotel, located next to the railroad tracks. In an era before mandatory smoke alarms, fire spread through the wood and brick structure, claiming five lives and destroyed the entire building. The fire also brought down the only hotel remaining in the community, and one has not been built since.

But there was a time when Cokato had as many as three hotels that stood ready to serve weary travelers passing through town.

James N. Runions opened his hotel in 1883. Runions was an original settler in Cokato, an influential businessman, and street commissioner (which in that era meant making sure the mud did not get too deep in the streets during the spring). Runions hotel was, as Carlton Lee described it, "a showplace in its time."

One block away was the Western House, run by the brother and sister pair of Charles (C. M.) and Carrie Carlson, which opened in 1888. Later, this building was purchased and used by Johnson Produce, and now is owned by Reed Carlson (its current tenants include the MAWSECO offices).

Both hotels were a short walking distance from the railroad depot and featured all the amenities required of their patrons.

Traveling salesman were frequent residents of both hotels. Each featured "Sample Rooms," where merchants were free to inspect the products these travelers brought with them, often in large wood trunks.

Both hotels also served as temporary residences for people who were working on the railroad or hired for temporary jobs in town. Many new immigrants would spend their first few days under Runions or Carlson's roofs. (Last summer a family from Sweden brought in a letter from one of their ancestors that was written on Western House stationery. The letter described the man's journey to Cokato and his difficulty in finding work here.)

Competition between the two hotels was good-natured, but intense. Both Runions and Carlson would greet incoming passenger trains to solicit business. Runions was, as Frank Lamson described him, "a suave gentleman, well adapted to meeting the traveling public." Carlson, on the other hand, was not, and often found himself with no patrons to bring back with him.

Lamson also recalls a prank pulled on Runions by members of the Bachelor's Club, with the intention of lifting Carlson's sagging spirits.

One of the club's members (Dr. Tate) dressed as a woman, using a veil to cover his face. When the train arrived he (she) was approached by Runions who escorted him (her) to his hotel. Upon arriving at the hotel, Dr. Tate expressed dismay and noted that he (she) was supposed to meet a business associate at the Western House. Runions, being the gentleman he was, escorted the impostor to Carlson's hotel. Upon their arrival, Dr. Tate lifted his veil and exposed the ruse. Runions was reportedly angry, but did not retaliate against the pranksters.

Both hotels were also social centers in the community. Wedding receptions, New Years Balls, and extravagant parties were just some of the activities that took place there.

The advent of car traffic would eventually cut into the rail passenger business the hotels depended upon. The Western House eventually closed. Runions would later sell his hotel to A. M. Atwood, who changed the name to Merchants Hotel. Later, it became the Cokato Hotel, which it remained until the fire in 1977.

Over two decades have passed since the fire and no hotel or motel has been built since. This may make one take pause to wonder if Cokato ever will see a day when travelers will find sanctuary here.

C. M. (Charles) & Carrie Carlson's Western House, corner of Millard Avenue & 2nd Street (across from the Great Northern Depot) , c1890.

James Runions hotel is at far left, partially obscured by the trees. This view was taken around 1910. The old village hall can be seen at the far right of the photo.

The Big Store

Its end was hardly worthy of how much of Cokato's life it had seen. Then again, sometimes it is far too easy to dispense with our past.

In October 1996, the building that stood near the corner of Third Street West and Millard Avenue came down. For most, it was a welcome end to what had become an eyesore. For others, it was a sad end to what had been one of Cokato's foremost businesses, run by one of the community's pioneer families.

The family name was Mabusth; and their long-time business, The Big Store.

For almost six decades, the Mabusth family and The Big Store served three generations of Cokato people and those who resided in the countryside.

Cokato Historical Society

In an era when people shopped in their own towns, The Big Store provided quality clothing-suits, hats, pants, boots, caps, shirts-and other dry goods typical of the time. Its merchandise displayed in a spacious show area, customers were recipients of nothing less than first-class service.

Upstairs from the store, there was a dance hall, meeting room, the home of the local Masonic lodge, and a small apartment. Certainly this fixture of Cokato's business district was a hub of activity.

At the time of his retirement in 1948, Big Store owner John J. Mabusth, was the oldest active member of the business community in Cokato, having entered that realm in 1889. Mabusth's obituary (July 9, 1953) noted that: "Many also recall that [he] showed personal interest in each customer, and was anxious that the patron be completely satisfied as to fit and quality of garments and footwear."

John J. Mabusth is buried in the Cokato Village Cemetery, along with his wife, parents, brother, and other community pioneers that helped transform Cokato from a small stop along the Great Northern Railroad into a thriving agricultural and retail center.

While no descendants of the Mabusth family reside in the Cokato area, many of them make regular visits to Cokato and the museum.

With so much of Cokato's downtown retail district a distant memory, the legacy of the Big Store and the Mabusth family is certainly worth noting.

Moons on Outhouse doors?

The answer lies in the lighting inside because outhouses were around before electricity. The best way to let light in was to put in a window. For privacy reasons, most outhouses were designed with the window above the line of sight. Many early outhouses contained a decorative "moon cutout" covered by glass. This allowed *just* enough light in to take care of business! It also allowed the real moon to shine through during the night. Most people had a covered pot under the bed to go in during the night.

Probably the most recognizable symbol associated symbol with the traditional outhouse building is the familiar crescent moon carved into the privy door. Actually, the symbol is an ancient one, and was a sign for womanhood in colonial days and on the frontier.

It's male counterpart, Sol, was either a star or a sun burst design also on the door. Since most male outhouses fell into disrepair rather quickly they seldom survived; while the female ones were better maintained, and were eventually used by both sexes. Although you can find outhouses still standing with the crescent moon, the original meaning for gender identification was lost by the later nineteenth century in most areas of the country.

The moon that is often found on the outhouse door stand for the ancient sign- luna- or womanhood. When the outhouse was first invented people needed these signs to discern which was the men's or women's bathroom-for most people couldn't read. Soon, however, the men's became rundown or was very unkempt and not maintained. So everybody just used the women's bathroom, and the men's sunburst or sol sign was forgotten. The moon sign was kept and is also used as a vent.

Corrected term of "quarter moon" as follows. The first sentence states that it is a quarter moon. A quarter moon, however, is a half lit moon where the terminator is half-way between each side of the disk. It would be more accurate to refer to the moon as a crescent moon in all cases. And if you wanted to be pedantic about it you could go so far as to call it a waxing or waning crescent moon depending on which side is lit.

Question: Is the crescent moon typically waxing or waning?

The answer: The moon is normally a Waning Crescent Moon.

A cobblers last

Photograph Index

REED
William Vernon Reed